"Vulnerable, hugely personal, unconventional, funny, engaging, provocative, unvarnished, sometimes raw, Steve Arterburn gets behind the eyelids and under the skin of men in midlife. Trust me, you won't lose interest."

— **Bob Buford**, Author of *Halftime* and *Finishing Well*

"Every page of this book spoke directly to me. I laughed out loud, while at other times got really, really quiet and reflective. Since reading this book I can't stop thinking about it. It's helpful, practical, challenging, and worth your time."

— **Jim Burns, PhD**, President of HomeWord and
   Author of *Creating an Intimate Marriage* and *Confident Parenting*

"What a timely book! Every man in midlife needs to read this manual. It's vulnerable, practical, and biblical. Best of all, it will show you how the best is yet to come!"

— **Les Parrott, PhD**, Founder of RealRelationships.com
   and Author of *Your Time-Starved Marriage*

"Steve Arterburn is the most qualified man I know to speak to the life transitions of men. I have seen him live out the principles of this book with my own eyes and sought, through imitation, to navigate my journey as a man in similar ways. He has never done me wrong as a man. Join me!"

— **Kenny Luck**, Men's Pastor of Saddleback Church
   and Author of *Every Man, God's Man; RISK; DREAM;*
   and *FIGHT*

"Thanks, Steve and John, for telling us to take a minute, shut off the 'autopilot,' and think about how to live the second half. If more men would do what this book says, the midlife crises would change to midlife corrections and the second half could be much better than the first!"

—**Dr. Henry Cloud**, Psychologist and Author

"Finally there's help for men at that dangerous midlife crossroad in life. Steve Arterburn and John Shore outline for us how a man can make a smooth transition through midlife and avoid the midlife crisis that ruins so many men."

—**Dave Stoop, PhD**, Psychologist and Author

"Steve and I have shared many hours together laughing and sharing and reaching out to others. This midlife manual is full of great wisdom and will be a real help to men who want to soar through midlife rather than crash in a crisis."

—**Josh D. McDowell**, Author and Speaker

"The middle years can often be a bewildering and even disappointing time for men. However, it doesn't have to be that way. With Steve Arterburn's sound and clear guidance, these can truly be our best years. Steve combines years of experience in helping others with his own personal authenticity and a solid biblical base. You will be a better person for reading this book."

—**Dr. John Townsend**, Psychologist, Author, and Speaker

Midlife Manual for Men

FINDING SIGNIFICANCE IN THE SECOND HALF

Stephen Arterburn
and John Shore

MIDLIFE
MANUAL
FOR MEN

BETHANYHOUSE
MINNEAPOLIS, MINNESOTA

a division of Baker Publishing Group

Published by Bethany House Publishers
11400 Hampshire Avenue South
Bloomington, Minnesota 55438

Bethany House Publishers is a division of
Baker Publishing Group, Grand Rapids, Michigan

Printed in the United States of America

ISBN 978-0-7642-0661-0

The Library of Congress has cataloged the hardcover edition as follows:

Arterburn, Stephen, date.
    Midlife manual for men : finding significance in the second half. / Stephen Arterburn and John Shore.
        p.   cm. — (Life transitions)
    Summary: "Written for men in midlife, to help them first examine the roles they have in life, including husband, father, and provider, and then give them the tools to make the rest of their lives matter"—Provided by publisher.
    ISBN-13: 978-0-7642-0423-4 (hardcover : alk. paper)
    1. Middle-aged men—United States—Psychology. I. Shore, John, date– II. Title.
    HQ1059.5.U5A78   2008
    305.244—dc22

                                                                    2007036388

To Larry Sonnenburg, the most amazing husband,
father, leader, and friend.
S.A.

For Dad and Mom.
J.S.

CONTENTS

Midlife Manual for Men

INTRODUCTION

IT HAPPENS TO everyone fortunate enough to live long enough. Sooner or later, we all experience that wake-up call that explodes like a bomb in the gut. Boom! — and then you know it: You really are middle-aged. People having that moment tend to do a nanosecond evaluation of their life. And that's usually all it takes for them to realize that they wish they had done more, lived more, been more. If you have experienced that moment yourself—or think it might be a good idea to prepare for when you do—then this is the right book for you.

As you surely know, if you were born anywhere from around 1946 to 1964, you're officially a "baby boomer." In America today there are about thirty-nine million guy boomers. (*Man,* but that's a lot of testosterone let loose upon the world at one time. In one disgusting way or another, it probably helps explain global warming.) We, your authors Steve and John, are both in our early fifties. That puts us solidly in the middle of the Boomer Horde.

Go boomers!

Whoo-hoo!

It's good to belong, isn't it?

Of course, people of our generation are, by nature, Rebellious Types. We *know* from rebellion, man. Rebellion is what our generation *did*.

Wait. Didn't we? We did, right? Mostly? Some?

Hmmm. We seem to recall something about the Beatles, the first man on the moon, yo-yos, and polyester jumpsuits.

Was the first man on the moon Paul McCartney? Was he wearing a polyester jumpsuit and playing with a yo-yo?

It's all so hard to remember, isn't it?

Tell you what, though. The two of us sure know what's going on with ourselves *these* days.

These days, we're middle-aged.

Us!

You!

All thirty-nine million of us!

Middle-aged!

It's just too weird to think about.

And it's *certainly* too weird not to.

Midlife is such a glorious, scary time of life, isn't it?

And that's what we want to talk to you about—about every way in which midlife is both glorious and scary, and how it's so much more than either. We wrote this book because we want to share with you the comprehensive, God-inspired understanding that we've come to about men in midlife. We wanted to provide you with an owner's manual, if you will, for the rest of your life.

Midlife raises a lot of questions. Though we know it sounds presumptuous to say so, we believe this book contains the answers to those questions.

So let's get started!

We're men!

We're not big on waiting!

With appreciation for letting us share in your midlife adventure,

Steve and John

MAN IN THE MIDDLE | 1

FROM STEVE:

I miss a lot. I have a true case of attention deficit disorder, and I don't just use it as a lame excuse for doing some really dumb things. It is, for me, the real deal, and it is quite painful at times having to deal with the consequences of things like crashing cars because I'm so easily distracted, or talking to someone and having no idea what they've been saying for the past five minutes, or speaking to an audience in one city while *thinking* that I'm speaking to a different audience in an altogether different city.

Can you imagine standing before a group of building contractors in Las Vegas, giving the talk you had *intended* to present the following week to residents of the Los Angeles Mission?

That happened to me once, and believe me, you learn to think *fast* in a situation like that; I had to instantly turn a speech meant for homeless people into a speech delivered to contractors about the true value of a home. (It worked: My audience was in tears!) Such is my life of missing things. (I can't leave this tangent without mentioning that I once spent a week, in the dead of winter, at St. Thomas University, just outside Albany, New York. Too bad I wasn't at the St. Thomas University of the Virgin Islands—where I *thought* I had agreed to speak. I had packed my sandals, shorts, and shades and was ready for white sands and ocean waves. Instead, I got white snow and waves of depression.)

My attention problem has become so bad that I pay extra for a GPS device (Hertz calls them NeverLost) whenever I rent a car, because I simply cannot drive, read a map, and get anywhere on time. The GPS system was to be my salvation; and it has helped, but I can still sometimes have a tough time knowing what to do. Just this morning, for instance, in Bozeman, Montana (I write on planes), I approached an intersection as the GPS lady said, "Turn in point three miles"—and I did not know whether to turn at the intersection I was just nearing, believe that there would be another intersection farther ahead, or what. As a result of this type of navigational crisis, one of the most common phrases running through my head these days is "recalculating route." "Recalculating route" is repeated so much by the lady in the GPS box that I expect to go to my car one morning and hear a male voice telling me the lady quit because she got tired of my not following directions.

Such fears can make for a difficult way of life.

One night, while lying in bed counting penguins jumping off an iceberg into the water (I'm old; sheep don't work for me anymore), this "recalculating route" phrase kept interrupting my Penguin Parade. And then it hit me just how much a GPS device is like God: He never abandons us or gives up on us; he is always there—no matter how far off course we are—waiting to *recalculate the route*. I love that about God. Never too late, never too early to get us back on track. In a nutshell, that is what this book is about: letting God recalculate your route to get you from where you are to the best days of your life.

Recalculation can begin with a decision, but it often takes a crisis to get our attention. At least, that is what my distracted mind apparently needed. When my world came falling apart, it was like I was dead. Heavy, cold air pressed in around me. My folded hands were resting on my chest as I lay flat on my back on a couch that felt more like a coffin. It was the middle of the night. Everything, seemingly everywhere, was perfectly still. With every breath I felt my chest expanding and contracting. Beyond that I wasn't feeling anything at all. Everything was vacuous, hollow, empty.

Feeling takes awareness. Awareness takes an identity. My identity had been blown apart by a bomb I can still feel today. *BOOM!* Then everything was different.

My wife of seventeen years had left me. Our daughter, whom I love so much, could not have been at a more vulnerable age. She was eleven, and I hated having to tell her I could not fix this. Our home had become a house I didn't know. My life became a

succession of jerking, disconnected impressions of wildly vary-
ing intensities. I didn't always know what I was feeling, but I
know it always hurt.

Awake I felt like a ghost, a too-real phantom in someone
else's dream. Asleep I dreamed I was awake, and falling with
no net. Not only was my marriage ending, but I also thought
my work, my ministry, my *raison d'être* were also over—all of
it, dead and unsalvageable.

I was forty-six years old. I was as miserable as I'd ever been
in my life.

It was one of the few times I felt no hope. None.

It's an understatement to say that I had some emotional
work to do. And the work began that night on my knees. Everything had been stripped from me, including pretense and super-
ficiality. It was all real; and *I* was as real as I have ever been. It
was just me and Jesus—fellowshiping in suffering.

More than six years later, happiness is both an everyday and
an all-new experience for me. I'm now married to a woman I
love very much, who is *literally* the answer to my prayers. Misty
and I have a one-year-old son, Solomon, along with my daughter,
Madeline, and Misty's two boys, Carter and James. It is a very
fun and loving family.

By remaining open to what God began telling me that desperate night and by staying connected to healthy people, my
life has become something better than anything I would have
then dared to imagine for myself.

And I was afraid middle age would be, of all things, boring.

One of the most wonderful things about being in midlife today is the sheer time it leaves us to reflect upon, adjust, or change our lives. In the year 1800, life expectancy for an American man was thirty-five years.

In 1900, the average life expectancy was forty-six years.

In 1950, it was sixty-nine.

Today, the average life expectancy for a man is seventy-six years old. So you literally could say that seventy-six is the new thirty-five.

Besides reminding us that we have much to be grateful for, these facts show that those of us who are actually in midlife are going through something that's truly unprecedented. Never in history have so many people at one time had to deal with what it really *means* to be, say, forty-five years old and know that you might very well still have half your life ahead of you. The uniqueness of that situation sheds light on the reason so many of us don't feel anywhere near as old as our chronological age. In fact, the other day, when I was speaking to a group of "twentys," I told them what fun it was for me to speak to people who are the same age as I feel. They laughed (the whippersnappers), but it was completely true.

Our feeling that way makes perfect sense, doesn't it? Because the model that we have in our heads of what it *means* to be fifty years old is the people our parents were—or, worse, the people their parents were—when *they* were fifty.

Our parents at fifty seemed a lot older than we feel at fifty. And I don't think it's just because men's hair was oiled and women's ratted—or that any of their wardrobes would be featured today on *What Not to Wear*. No, they seemed older because in every physical way our parents *were* older at fifty than we are or will be at the same age. And we know that's true because we know that overall their generation's life expectancy is lower than ours. (And they were modeling *their* midlife on what our grandparents were like at forty-five or fifty. To our parents, forty-five or fifty meant you were *truly* old.)

At fifty, I felt like I was just getting started—and I still feel that way today. And with a one-year-old, that's a very good thing indeed.

The bottom line is that by every possible measure we are simply not as physically or mentally aged as our parents or grand-parents were when they were as old as we are now.

It's more than just a cliché. Sixty really is the new fifty. Fifty really is the new forty—and forty really is the new thirty.

And that means that all of us who are middle-aged today really are (whether boldly or not) going where no man has ever gone before.

And that can be a little disorienting.

Signs of the Times

Each man going through midlife right now will respond to that extremely personal journey in a way unique to himself. For some guys, midlife means watching their diet and joining a gym. For others, it means shaving their head, getting a tattoo, and trying to join their nephew's college fraternity. For some it becomes a time for "performance enhancing drugs" such as

Viagra and Cialis. (I thank God for the advances in pharmacology such as these—well, and of course for those that do so much to fight other conditions, such as diabetes and psoriasis.) Most of us take the simpler route to midlife: We just start losing our hair and try to prevent parting what's left of it in a circle, or start combing it with a washcloth with the use of a "follicle enhancing" drug like Propecia or Rogaine.

For the majority of guys, midlife is an experience to be ranked on a scale somewhere between "a cake walk" and a "trip to hell and back." In other words, chances are you are reading this book because you have a desire to take some stock of your life, recalculate your priorities, and position yourself to have a great "second half." Most of you are not in free fall, feeling like your entire world is coming apart—but maybe you do believe that certain pieces of it are indeed fraying at the ends. Maybe you know you've made mistakes along the way, and that you're carrying some bags on your back with labels like "unfulfilled dreams," "regrets," "disillusionment," or "guilt." And you know what? We are too! The good news is, it's time to lose the baggage and grab hold of the amazing (though not always easy) things God has in store for you at this phase of the journey.

In other words, you're normal—whatever "normal" is, other than a midsized city in Illinois.

So it's time to learn how to pack lightly, gentlemen, because on the trip we're taking, there's only room for a couple of light carryons. As you'll see, previous sins, gaffs, screw-ups, regrets, and guilt fit neither under the seat in front of you nor in God's overhead compartment. (Whatever that means—heaven maybe?

We really don't know. It's just an analogy; it's best not to think too much about it.)

Anyway, some of us do get thoroughly lost in the trip that is midlife. For that reason it's good to be aware of the signs that show when a man has strayed precariously off course. Again, you may not personally be experiencing any of the following symptoms, but perhaps you know someone who is. These are the sorts of things men typically suffer when they slide into that emotionally chaotic time we often call a "midlife crisis" (which, of course, can occur at any time, even though it might be identified as a quarter-life or three-quarters-of-life crisis; no matter what you call it—it's a crisis).

Sustained Depression

As you may or may not know (and we pray you don't), sustained depression hurts like nothing in this world. If you've ever suffered from this particularly malicious infirmity, you know it's that grueling, relentlessly dark state where you . . . well, where you can barely function at all; where you would be painfully aware of your tragically low self-esteem, if only thinking about it at all didn't take so much energy. Indeed, just thinking about thinking makes you want to turn up the TV. This is the Life Lock where you do, in fact, watch a lot of TV, eat a lot of garbage, and snarl at people who come anywhere near you—especially if (God help them) they try to help. The depression a man in midlife can suffer is often fueled by his conviction that he is chronically and profoundly underappreciated or underachieving, or only valued for what he achieves. It's truly a bad place to be.

If you think you or someone you know is suffering from genuine, clinical depression, we implore you to reach out and enlist the help of a qualified counselor. According to the American Psychiatric Association, the symptoms of a depression serious enough to need professional help are

- changes in appetite or sleeping patterns
- loss of interest in former activities
- general fatigue
- feelings of worthlessness or hopelessness
- feelings of guilt
- an inability to think, concentrate, or make decisions
- a preoccupation with death or suicide
- a manifest sadness or grief
- constant physical ailments such as headaches or stomachaches

I would add to this list, based on my own experience, impotence (that's right, that's when I learned about the power of Cialis) and a deep sense of inadequacy and incompetence. And finally—the deep-seated desire to turn out all the lights, draw the blinds, and lie in bed sleeping or trying to.

Restlessness

This is where, rather abruptly, you become something of a Tasmanian devil. Everything's exciting; everywhere you look, you see unbelievable potential. Suddenly you have all kinds of new friends and associates that you find fascinating. All the regular,

everyday stuff in your life now seems dull, each another indica-
tor of a rut so deep and long it's as if you've awakened from a
dream in which you were a huge, blind mole digging your way
into your eventual grave. You want out, so you head straight
up and bust through the ground and into the sun—enthralled
by this bright new world and all the new people you've found
in it, *great* people who have all these *great* new ideas, ways,
and allurements! *Yippee!* Fun! (Or at least it *would* be fun, if
it wasn't such a fleeting state of mind that tries to compensate
for everything but accomplishes nothing except to plummet you
deeper into the dark chasm of depression.)

Midlife crisis?! *What midlife crisis?!*

Acute Irritability

There is nothing cute about an irritable man. This trait in
a man can be difficult to isolate and identify, since, let's face it,
in general men do tend to be a tad fairly short-tempered. It's
not that we *mean* to be mean, of course. It's just that for some
reason known only to him, the good Lord above has seen fit to
populate the lives of each and every one of us down here with
more boneheaded morons than any human being should ever
have to meet in the course of his entire *life*, much less have to
deal with on a day-to-day basis. So of course it's only natural,
isn't it, that at times, while having to deal with the continuous,
egregious inadequacies of others, any man's patience should
run a smidgen thin. But that everyday, run-of-the-mill snarki-
ness isn't the kind of irritability we're talking about here. This
Persistent Middle-Age Fury is the kind that causes your wife to

cry, your kids to storm out of the house, and your co-workers to say loudly enough for everyone to hear, "What's your problem, anyway?" Problem is, you can't do anything about your cranky responses to just about anything that moves—and you aren't even all that sure you want to, either. Not good.

Way Too Much "Partying"

When did "party" become a verb—and one meaning "to get high," at that?

Oh right. About thirty years ago.

Of course, most men don't struggle with substance abuse. But it can be a temptation for a man who has been knocked far enough off his bearings that he is, in this way, driven to get even *more* lost than he already is. It's a difficult and most painful trap to get snared in. What makes it worse is that once a person has begun abusing alcohol or drugs, he's usually closed off to any sort of advice or counsel. Even so, Mr. Party Hearty needs your reality check. While it won't make you popular with him, let him know that when he is finished with putting off the pain and ready to face it and work through it, you are ready to help him find the best source of help.

Endangering Your Finances

Again, this is pretty atypical behavior. But for some of us, there's something about the pressing of midlife that can really make a guy want to buy all kinds of things that he wouldn't dare to if being middle-aged hadn't caused him to go a little (or a lot) nuts. The red sports car is, of course, the classic Midlife Guy

Acquisition, but that's really more of a stereotype than a reality. The sports car doesn't have to be red. It can also be silver. Or black. Or blue! Especially that really dark midnight blue, with the high-gloss sheen, and the embedded little gold specks that catch the light just so. For me, it was a yellow convertible with a brown top so beautiful people would applaud at traffic lights. I bought it on the "buy before you die" plan even though I had only hit the big four-zero.

Wait . . . where were we?

Oh right: Guys caught in the throes of a midlife crisis sometimes become . . . well, money hogs, basically. Sailboats; the complete line of Eddie Van Halen electric guitar equipment; a home theater system so humongous that if you took the roof off your house guys passing by in the space shuttle could watch *Braveheart* along with you; a bar; a tropical island; a ten-gallon hat . . . Price-wise, of course, it's all relative. And without question it's the sort of thing that makes people who run credit card companies stay awake nights, rubbing their hands and giggling maniacally. Having watched this phenomenon over the years and having participated in it, the trend seems to be that the less connected in relationships men are, the more connected they become to things.

Becoming Obsessed With Sex

As you are (alas) no doubt aware, when it comes to sex, many of us retain certain . . . what's the word? . . . issues. For starters, we've given women every last reason to believe we men are—or certainly too often seem to be—essentially obsessed with sex. And for a lot of guys, midlife does *not* help with the problem of an overactive sexual imagination, with fantasizing about women other than their wives. It sure can exacerbate that problem, though. A guy feels his life is half over, and then BOOM!—he does the unthinkable: He commits the worst of the worst sin, and he has no idea that it was compensation behavior, that he was only trying to prove he still had it. And in the wake of acting out come broken dreams and heartaches. Fortunately, today more than at any other time, men are taking steps to prevent the midlife crisis from becoming a sexual betrayal. But there are still those who just don't see it coming—like the pastor I met last week who became a competition salsa dancer—amazingly, at the age of forty. Right on schedule.

Poor God. The things he must hear.

And see.

And shake his head at.

And, no doubt, root for us to outgrow, or finally work out before anyone gets hurt.

Having an Affair

This is where the fantasies very often rooted and nurtured in the hothouse of Midlife Imaginations blossom forth into the ultimate Flytrap *a la* Venus (or another word that, um, rhymes with "Venus").

Verily, this is the mother of all midlife crisis symptoms.

And if you're a married guy who is having—or who's had—an affair, please tune in completely to what I am about to say:

Trust that as dark a time as this is for you and your wife, a bright new dawn is possible—and later in this book we'll talk about what exactly you can do to initiate and give rise to that new day. For now, though, let us say you must tell your wife about that affair, and soon. She deserves to know.

And the best time to tell her is after you have told the "other" woman it is over and after you have gotten involved in some kind of treatment. I don't know what you paid for this book, but the advice right here is worth the money. What you *must* do is flat-out decide whether you are planning to stay with your wife or leave her. If the latter, allow me to tell you what is ahead. First of all, the woman you are sleeping with idealized you and thinks you are amazing, wonderful, and everything she has ever wanted. Now realize she thinks that about a man who lies to his wife, breaks his wife's heart, and cannot be trusted. But she will overlook all of that until the Elvis impersonator sings something originally sung by the Carpenters in a Las Vegas chapel. Once she has you, she will own you, and you will be amazed at how quickly you will become inadequate to meet her needs. You will be walking around mumbling to yourself what thousands of other men have mumbled after they did the same stupid thing you did: *"What* have I *done?"* You will have lost your reputation, re-spect from your kids, and the belief that you really did have integrity—all for a woman who will very quickly treat you just like your wife did, because that is the kind of treatment you either draw out of women or drive them to. So if you are in a pre-midlife, midlife, or post-midlife affair, you need to follow the instructions exactly as I give them below:

1. Call, do not see in person, the other woman, and tell her you realize you have been going down the wrong path in many areas of your life, and you are sorry you got her involved. Ask her to forgive you, then tell her it is over and that you will not phone, email, call, or come to see her and that you want her to move on with her life.

2. Change your cell phone number and email address.

3. Call 1-800-NEW-LIFE, tell them what you have done, ask them to recommend to you a male counselor in your area—and then start going to see that counselor.

4. Do any or (best!) all of the following: Go to an Every Man's Battle workshop; join a Celebrate Recovery group; and/or attend a Sex Addicts Anonymous meeting.

5. Under the guidance of your counselor, pick the right time to confess to your wife.

6. Email me at *SArterburn@newlife.com* and thank me.

Optional: When you wake up one day and realize that I helped you dodge not a bullet but a heat-seeking missile, out of gratitude become a supporter of New Life Ministries.

Ground Control: We Have a Problem

Most guys going through midlife don't, of course, become severely depressed, constantly enraged, drug-taking, sex-obsessed spendthrifts who sleep around. But even the most well-adjusted among us are prone to feeling tweaked by the way midlife seems to loosen so many of the fasteners that have for so long kept our lives intact.

It can start feeling like we no longer control the stuff over which we've always had so *much* control.

Like, for instance . . . let's see . . . oh, let's just pick any example—like, say, what happens in midlife *to our entire body*?

Isn't what happens to your body in midlife just so . . . *rude,* basically? One minute your body's a perfectly serviceable comrade in arms—going where you want it to go, doing what you want it to do, generally following orders. It looks good when you dress it up; people aren't too readily inclined to scream or faint when they see it; everything on it remains pretty much as it's always been. It's all right.

And then, all of a sudden, it's sort of . . . not.

I (Steve here) am reminded of a time when I recently arrived at my friend Glen's house to pick him up for a trip we were taking together. I found him sunk deep into an oversized armchair. He looked decidedly morose.

"What's wrong?" I asked. "Is everything all right?"

Unmoving, Glen looked up at me. "Everything was just fine," he said, "until this morning." He shook his head sadly.

"What is it?" I said. "What happened?"

"Well, I was getting out of the shower maybe a half hour ago, and just toweling off, as usual. So, you know how we put those new mirrors in our bathroom?" I nodded. Recently, Glen and his wife had installed a new high bank of mirrors all along the wall behind the sinks in their master bathroom.

"So?" I said. "Did the mirrors fall off or something? Humidity get to 'em?"

Glen snorted. "I wish they'd fallen off. But no. Oh no. They stayed there. They work perfectly." His voice became a tad manic. "So I was drying off, right? And I was looking at myself in these giant mirrors, and . . . and that's when it happened." He sighed. "I was standin' there, doing the ol' back-drying thing—you know, where you saw the towel back and forth behind you? And then I stopped doing that, you know? Like, I was done moving. Except that my body kept on going!" Glen's voice rose to a pitch approaching desperation. "I stopped. I'm done; I'm entirely not moving anymore—but I see in the mirror that my body's not even *close* to being still. And there was nothing I could do but watch! I felt like a chunk of banana staring out from the middle of a bowl of Jell-O someone had just wobbled. It was horrible!"

Though I didn't mean to laugh at my friend's distress, I couldn't help but crack a smile. Glen saw it and started laughing.

"What happened to the guy I used to be?" he said. "And when did mirrors get so cruel? And why didn't you tell me my back was getting so fat? You always say, 'Glen, I got your back,' but if that was true, you would have told me my back had more fat than you can find on a sperm whale."

Life.

It sure can creep up on a person, can't it?

Especially from the back.

Back to the Future

Midlife can feel like it has not only crept up on you, but like it has mugged you. If you've ever felt astonished to find yourself in middle age, one of the big reasons is probably because you've spent the last forty or fifty years being so extraordinarily busy that you simply haven't had much time to stop and think about where you are relative to the entirety of your life span.

And you've also probably never been particularly motivated to think about that sort of stuff. Why would you be? You were young! For the young, there's always tomorrow.

Then one day—right around, say, your fortieth birthday—it begins to dawn on you that instead of being infinite, the number of your available tomorrows is terribly finite. At one point or another along the journey of your life, you come around a bend and see, on the far side of the vast field into which your path disappears into the grass, the Grim Reaper.

There he is, looking directly at you . . . waving a big, boney-armed hello.

And *that* is when most guys stop in their tracks. The awareness of our mortality kicks in with an urgency it previously lacked. And that urgency compels us to do a lot of things—some of the more extreme examples of which we looked at earlier in this chapter. But the chief and most common response is to begin to think very hard about the kind of person we are, have been, and want to be.

And thinking about *that* can sure . . . keep a guy awake at night. Because if you're a Christian, you're acutely aware of the quality of the man you most definitely *want* to be when you hear what Shakespeare called the "knell that summons thee to heaven or to hell." And that man, of course, is someone who is pleasing to the Lord.

We all want different individual things out of our lives, but in the end what all of us want most is to be confident that when in the afterlife we come into the bodily presence of Jesus himself, he really *does* smile at us, put his hand upon our shoulder, and say, "Well done, good and faithful servant."

If we're honest, though, most of us don't feel absolutely 100 percent *positive* that we're worthy of such judgment. And even if we feel sure that we are—even if by some miracle of self-esteem we harbor no doubts whatsoever about the quality of our character—we still very much want to spend the second half of our lives here on earth in a way that fully glorifies God.

So. That's what we're here to make sure happens.

And we have a way!

And that way involves looking not (at first) to the future, but to the past.

You know: Looking back at all the years that we've spent being so radically, joyously, frightfully, crazily *busy*.

The only way to get to a certain place is to know where you're starting from, right? And you can't really know where you're *at* unless you know how you got there.

Plus, you can't reflect upon your life by looking at the future. Unless you're . . . Nostradamus. Which you're *not*. So that settles it.

To the past it is!

The Roles of a Lifetime

When from the crest of the formidable speed bump that is midlife we look back on our lives, most of us see that what we've been so busy doing with our lives is our absolute darndest to successfully fulfill—or perhaps just *survive*—what amounts to four distinct Life Roles: that of Son, Husband, Provider, and Father. These are the Life Roles that most of us at first simply inhabit, and then (less simply) become.

So remember, guys: It's Roles, Inhabit, Become. Or RIB—as in what Adam discovered he was missing just before *his* big life role became Just Like Eve, But Different. (And don't forget: We are all members of *the* Adam's Family.)

Here's the thing, though, about those four Manliest of Roles: By midlife, they have radically and permanently changed. What in one way or another wakes and shakes up every man in midlife is the dawning truth that he can no longer continue to be the only person he's spent his entire life learning how to be.

We've learned how to be good sons—but then find that our parents need us to care or provide for them.

We've learned how to be good husbands—but then the bodies and sexuality (to name but two aspects) of both ourselves and our wives change into something with which we have no experience at all.

We've learned how to be good providers—but then find that we're becoming obsolete in the workplace, or we realize that the careers we've spent so long carving for ourselves have almost nothing to do with what we've always *really* wanted to do with our lives, or we've simply become painfully bored with our jobs. Or maybe we just want to retire—and yet can barely imagine what that actually means.

We've learned how to be good fathers to our children—and then discover that, alas, our children are children no more.

So here we are, in a life that's clearly become a production radically different from the one in which we're used to starring. Suddenly, it seems as if everybody's character in the show has changed and nobody's sticking to the script; the action's not like anything we've rehearsed before. Pieces of the set are getting dragged off into the wings, lights are blinking all over the place—all *kinds* of things are going on that we've never even almost experienced.

Pretty exciting!

Pretty unnerving!

And, we would like to suggest, in every last way, wonderful. The whole thing is just great. Because we believe that it's in our middle age that God intends for us to stop, look back at the roles we've played thus far, and see if we can't find within them every last thing we need in order to create for ourselves, with his help and guidance, the very life that he most wants us to have.

So. We're going to spend the next five chapters talking about how we might most fruitfully go about that most precious and vital of explorations.

To help us cull the Right Stuff from each of the four primary roles of our lives, we will, in the chapter devoted to each role, follow the same four-step process.

First, under Good Riddance, we'll look at the aspects of that role that quite often prove *less* than entirely healthy for us. These will be the negative aspects of each role that we would do well to identify and then jettison.

Next, under Pure Gold, we'll take stock of those aspects of that role that have typically been *good* for us: that tended to ennoble us, strengthen us, make us better, wiser, more pleasing to God. This is the stuff about that role which we should hold on to and build upon as we move into the second half of our lives.

Under the next section of each chapter, Movin' On, we'll consider how we might use the best of what that role taught us—the "gold" that we just identified—to fashion for ourselves the kind of life that we've always dreamed of having.

Finally, under Things to Do, we'll offer suggestions and exercises designed to enhance your experience and appreciation of what was covered in that chapter. Do whichever of these exercises feels comfortable to you, secure in the knowledge that if you don't do every single one of them God will strike you down for your lackadaisical attitude toward him, your family, your community, your church, and your very own self.

Men.

Say about us what you will, but you can't say we're not funny.

Okay—you can't say that we don't *try* to be funny.

Anyway, back to business.

Let's begin!

Except, not yet. Before moving on to our four specific life roles of Son, Husband, Provider, and Father, let us first stop to treat as a role the original, fundamental *uber-role* that can dominate and most certainly informs just about everything that we men ever do in our lives at all.

HE-MAN OF THE UNIVERSE | 2

AT THIS POINT we ask every man reading this book to place one hand on your heart and read aloud the following official He-Man of the Universe pledge:

I [insert name, or totally cool nickname you know you deserve], being of what I think is an exceptionally sound mind and a still reasonably functional body, do hereby pledge that I, and I alone, have at one time or another viewed myself as the ultimate and unarguably supreme He-Man of the Universe. Thus was I born; thus have I lived this life; thus will I spend the next. Whether or not my mother adored me with passion inexhaustible, or whether or not as a child did my wondrous and sundry powers alternately cause my father to quake with fear and swell with pride, I have always believed that I am a special and unique gift to the world.

There were times when all who knew me delighted in my presence. Even today, some find me downright aphrodisiacal: physically irresistible, breathtakingly intelligent, enviably urbane. My sentiments are noble; my actions admirable; my thoughts sublime. I am also blessed with awesome hair, notwithstanding that of it which ultimately became follicle fun for frustratingly fickle Fate. The locus of my indomitable strength and power is not my heart or feelings. It is my Testosterone Manufacturing Power Plant. Testosterone is that most vital and potent of the myriad homegrown hormones, that giver of verve, muscle, and a voice that rumbles like thunder! Hoorah for Testosterone! And now must someone fetch unto me the remote control, a ham and cheese on rye, and something frosty and frothy to drink. For sure am I that on some channel, somewhere, is being broadcast something or other it would please me to behold. And do also bring me some chips. Make them unto barbecue.

Okay. It is time to uncross your heart, disconnect from your self-obsession, and move on with me.

Now, wasn't that a good pledge? Didn't it sound a lot like what something inside of you *would* say?

You know it did.

You know that's a big part of who you are.

Admit it. It is.

We're men. It's . . . part of the package.

And it is the producer of a whole lot of *baggage*.

HE-MAN GOOD RIDDANCE #1:

The terrible burden of unceasing expectation
that comes with being He-Man of the Universe

Not too long ago John was at the San Diego Zoo, looking at some Malayan sun bears, when a father and son came and stood at the rail beside him. The boy was maybe seven; his father—who was wearing belted and pressed khaki shorts, a tucked-in printed T-shirt, and a baseball cap—looked to be in his early thirties. The boy pointed at the lolling creatures and asked his dad what kind of bears they were. Surprisingly, the dad then revealed himself to be a veritable Bear Expert.

"That's the *Helarctos malayanus*," pronounced the man sonorously. He then went on to give a considerable dissertation on what sun bears eat, where they live, how long they live, how much they typically weigh, and how, from where we were standing, we could tell which of the bears we were looking at were male or female.

The whole time the man was expounding, John kept his eyes on the bears, in order to take full advantage of the educational experience he'd happened upon.

What great luck! That guy really knew his bears!

Except, no, he didn't.

Situated in front of many displays at the San Diego Zoo are three-sided, rotatable, bullet-proof placards containing quite a bit of information about the animal before you. Near the end of the father's dissertation, John looked over at Professor Yogi

Bear and saw that he was secretly *reading* the sun bear's signage. Not that there was anything wrong with that, of course. But he was pretending like he *wasn't* reading it, holding his head as if he were looking straight ahead at the bears. Worse, he had actually positioned his body in such a way that it was clear he was trying to block his boy from knowing the rotating placard was there at all.

He was trying to trick his kid (and also John, I guess; it wasn't like he was whispering) into thinking that he just happened to be the world's leading expert on Malayan sun bears.

It was kind of cheesy of that man to do that, but the truth of the matter is that at one time or another we've all been either that father or his son. Pretending you know stuff you don't—or being lectured to by a grown-up man who seems to know what he's talking about but in fact doesn't—is just part of what it means to be a boy/man. Part of the emotional burden that all of us men carry with us is the pervasive, low-level conviction that *being* a man means we're supposed to

- know everything (or at least know more than the female we are trying to impress)
- be like a magnet to women (or at least intriguing enough for Christian women to want to know what category your spirit-controlled temperament falls into, and for non-Christian women to want to know your horror-scope sign)
- be in complete control of our emotions (or at least present a façade that emotions are a take-it-or-leave-it option)

- make a ton of money (or at least combine your income and credit up to your eyeballs to look like you could buy anything you wanted)
- be exceptionally wise (or at least talk like you're wise, by misquoting Scripture with an authoritative voice or by always saying "How interesting" when you have absolutely no idea what the brilliant woman you're with is talking about)
- be naturally athletic (or at least be an expert in one sport, even if it's water ballet or if you barely possess the athletic talent of a possum)
- never have anything not go exactly as you planned it (or at least be able to fake knowing where you are going, even when you come to a dead end after you have traveled from the desert to the sea, and are up some mountain at an altitude of fifteen thousand feet)
- not really mind physical pain (or at least be able to grit your teeth until you are alone and free to scream into a large pillow)
- know all about cars and machines in general (or at least be able to use some mechanical language, like "sprocket" or "adjustable anti-siphon piston ball cock") (In case that last part seems offensive, this is a real part, recently purchased and installed by my wife in our toilet. She was not in the toilet; the ball cock was.)
- be able to talk with animals (or at least seem to be interested in learning how to be more like the Dog Whisperer)

Okay, that last one might be a little out there, but you get the idea. For most of us, the bottom line on being a guy—a boy, a teenage boy, a young man, a man, a middle-aged man, an old man—is that it's almost always about . . . *machismo*. Being a Man's Man, strong and stoic. That is what we are, what we do. Or at least that is what most of us feel like we are supposed to be. It's an ideal that can hound us, insofar as we know we really can't live up to that intimidating Superman of a standard.

Jump higher. Run faster. See through walls.

Sure.

Meanwhile, we're idling in traffic and late for work, or we have tissue paper stuck all over our face from yet another one of our disastrous Quik-E-Shaves, or we have a wife who is deeply upset over how "emotionally unavailable" we always seem to be, or *something's* going on with us that makes it perfectly clear to whoever cares to notice that, far from being *super* anything, we're just . . . regular guys.

The Superman Standard is like a carrot forever dangling before us. And when you stop and think for a minute, we are paying a pretty high price to try to get that carrot—and carrots are not really all that great to begin with. Fortunately, middle age is a really good time to finally grasp that particular carrot—and to then drop it like yesterday's old, stinky carrot. Because it's garbage.

HE-MAN GOOD RIDDANCE #2:
Our enduring, ultimately crippling sense of entitlement

While Superman's powers derive from his being born on Krypton, the powers that lead your Average Joe here on earth to think of himself as a bit of a Superman (or at least like Clark Kent: someone who could *become* Superman) derive from his being born right here on the good ol' planet earth.

If there's one thing you can say about earth, it's that it's still very much a man's world, isn't it? And it was even more so back when we were kids—which is where we all got our basic view of the world and our role in it. It might not be right, but we guys rule. We may not, as in times gone by, rule via big clubs and heavy rocks we toss with alarming accuracy, but the fact remains that on the food chain that is life, men *are* the big dogs.

Whether we sense it or not, though, this power often fuels an undue sense of entitlement. Through no fault of our own— through the simple, omnipresent forces of socialization and as-sumed expectation—we come to believe that we truly deserve all of life's benefits, breaks, and gimme-gimmees.

It seems that in almost every culture there is a perception that turns into unfair practices of men being superior to women and entitled to more control, power, and privileges. Often, Chris-tian missionaries get a bad rap for contaminating cultures or "doing well financially while doing good for God." But what is consistent about their impact on cultures is that the truth

of the Bible often changed practices and elevated women to a
different place. Hawaii is an example. Before the missionaries,
women waited until the men finished eating and ate what was
left. The missionaries literally brought women to the table—and
they stayed there.

The fact remains, however, that power corrupts. And we
would submit that it's almost impossible for us who naturally
have so much power not to in some way become corrupted by it.
Is there a man among us who isn't aware that he too readily and
easily gets angry—that he's much quicker than he should be to
yell or lash out or in some way make his displeasure known? Isn't
it reasonable to guess that one reason we do such things—that
we act so childishly—is simply because we know that we can?
At a very deep level, we men tend to feel like we have the *right*
to act impatiently or dismissively or arrogantly—especially when
we're at home in our little . . . fiefdom. It's the same reason so
many of us have such a [insert very un-Christian word here] for
a boss; at work, that's *their* little fiefdom to rule as they please.
And all too very often, what pleases a man with power is to make
clear to his subordinates that, in his territory, he is king.

Our bosses (sometimes) do it; we (sometimes) do it; all guys
(sometimes) do it.

And when we do it—when we in any way take advantage
of whatever power we have—it means that we're forgetting, or
momentarily blocking out, him from whom all power derives:
God.

Not so good.

If something in the previous section caused a bit of a gulp to occur in your throat, you may want to take a look at my book *Reframe Your Life*. I begin by writing about one of the major life roadblocks as being arrogant entitlement, which is the opposite of humble willingness. Just the fact that you are reading this book shows you have some degree of willingness to take a second look at all of your life. *Reframe Your Life* will help you go deeper in this area of arrogance combined with entitlement.

HE-MAN GOOD RIDDANCE #3:
Suppressing our emotions

A favorite character type in movies is the ramblin', gun-slingin' martial artist motorcyclist who pulls onto a long lonely highway, just him and his dog named Dog on the back of the seat. He takes life on the chin, gives as good as he gets, and loves 'em and leaves 'em. And do you know what that guy's actually *thinking* as he's sitting on his bike, squintin' into the sun? He's thinking that he's only got about an eighth of a tank of gas left. He's thinking ol' Dog's come down with something that's making him stink something awful, and he's wondering whether he should take him to the vet or just wait it out. He's thinking that it's time to get a new pair of boots now that the sole of his right one has come apart under the toe and is flopping around.

He's thinking he should get a *job*.

If you ask him what he is *feeling*, though, forget it. He feels, but he does not know what it means to express or share a feeling other than anger. The man is worried, anxious, fearful, and just overall stressed. That is why his head does not move from side to side. The neck muscles are so tight that if he moved one way or the other, something might snap. So he looks straight ahead, like nothing in the world matters, while everything in life is starting to matter more and more.

Deep down inside, all of our iconic Strong and Silent types are full-on emotional basket cases. The reason they barely ever talk isn't because they're so perpetually cool and collected. They don't talk because they know if they do they'll start crying and whining in utterly career-destroying or image-breaking fashion. In our two-wheeler's mind, there is nothing worse than a mean hombre on a bike in tears.

You know how we're getting a new James Bond every seven years or so? That doesn't happen because the last actor playing that part decided to move on to other roles, or whatever. No. We keep getting new James Bondses because each *actual* James Bond keeps croaking from a heart attack. He can't take the stress that comes from constantly having to turn all of his emotions into exactly three: Grim, Condescending, and Condescendingly Grim.

It's not good for the James Bondses to do that with their emotions, and it's not good for us to do it with ours.

God gives us two ways to process and understand him and the world around us: through our thoughts and through our emotions. The thought part, we've got. Most guys are pretty good at thinking analytically, at rational analysis.

But when it comes to accessing and giving serious credibility to our emotions, we're sometimes a little too much in James Bondage, bound by an image that we think others want from us but that simply isn't working for us anymore.

Middle age is *the* time for a lot of us to let go of never letting go.

HE-MAN GOOD RIDDANCE #4:
Going it alone

When it comes to handling an intense personal issue, Plan A for most guys is Clam Up and Isolate. We men don't in general take pleasure from the company of others when we're trying to work out something that's very seriously just about us. In this (as in, let's face it, so many things) we're like animals: When the hurt is on, we're pretty much compelled by nature to crawl off into a dark, deep place where no one would even think to look for us so that we can basically curl up and . . . *be* with our hurt for a while. Bear down on it. See what the heck it really is.

Wait for it to kill us, even, if that's the way it's going to be.

Hey. We're men. We're ready to die if that's what it takes to . . . not have to talk to everybody and his cotton-pickin' brother about what's the matter with us.

As most of us know, Clam Up and Isolate does *not* describe the way women tend to handle emotional stress or pain. Generally speaking, when it comes to handling an acute emotional issue, women are inclined to "relate" about it or "share" it or "talk it out" or do something interactive with it.

Sometimes the Guy Way proves to be a perfectly adequate response to a personal problem. For instance, we (your authors) have a friend—a fellow we'll call Bud—who had a drinking problem. Great guy, wonderful wife and family, but he drank too much. He drank after work; he drank after dinner; he drank on weekends. He never lost control of himself or anything close to it, but he wasn't exactly Ward Cleaver. So one day Bud's kids and wife sat him down at the family dinner table and lovingly told him that they too often felt like his beer meant more to him than they did, and how much that hurt them. They told him that they felt like his drinking meant that he just didn't really ever want to *be* there for them. And they reminded him of all the times that, in fact, he wasn't.

With tears in his eyes, Bud looked at his family and said, "This is terrible. I can't have this. You guys know how much I love you. I'm sorry about this. Let me fix it."

Then Bud took some food, some soda, and went into his rec room—a room he'd built onto his house where he kept an old couch, a television, a dart board, and so on; he and his buddies sometimes hung out there to watch football and smoke cigars and be Generally Manly about everything.

Bud went into his rec room, closed the door behind him, and didn't come out for three days.

And between then and now, Bud has never touched a drop of alcohol.

Problem solved. Bud never talked about what he did in that room or what he thought about in there or anything. He just stopped, on a dime, behavior that he'd habitually engaged in for twenty-some years.

So there's an example of a time when the Guy Way worked. That's pretty rare, though. Most guys taking Bud's approach would have emerged from that room with the exact same problem they had going into it. It's just hard to get the perspective necessary to clear up your own emotional problems and dependencies. When it comes to working out emotional problems, our women are generally (gee, what a surprise) very right indeed: We men *do* need to discuss our troubles with the people in our lives who mean the most to us.

Which, for most of us, means our wives.

So remember: Whenever something's really eating at you, the lesson here is to talk out your problems with your wife, or someone else you're close to. The lesson is *not* that you should build a rec room onto your house. That's not what we're saying.

Seriously. We're not. It's *not* about the rec room.

Okay, just forget about Bud, all right?

C'mon, man. Put down the hammer.

Now that we have addressed a few things that can stand in your way of being a real man in a real world with real connections with real people, let's look at some positives about coming into your own as a man.

HE-MAN PURE GOLD #1:
Your understanding of the nature of power

Earlier we talked about the downside of our having so much power in life. Here comes the *up*side. As boys, we learned that men have the most power in this world; as men, we've learned to live with what that really means.

For one thing, a lot of times the proverbial buck really *does* stop with us. We are very often the default winner in the "Who's Going to Step Up?" competition. If someone's trying to break into our house in the middle of the night, for instance, it's not our children or wife who are expected to grab a baseball bat and go out there and see whether the intruder can be convinced that he's chosen the wrong house. If there's a cataclysmic event, and suddenly food or water becomes terribly scarce, who's supposed to venture into the streets and make sure they come back with whatever's necessary to keep everyone back home alive?

That's right: Dog. About time that animal did something for us for a change, right?

No: It's us. Of course it's us. *We're* supposed to do All Things Manly. And that, as we all know, covers an awful wide range of territories.

Which is certainly *not* to say, by the way, that women can't protect themselves, their families, or their homes. Of course they can—and if any woman feels that she cannot, we pray she comes to understand that she's mistaken, and then takes whatever steps she needs to become secure in the knowledge that she can be just as lethal as any man. (One time John taught a self-defense class for women at a local Y. Talk about a lesson in unwarranted gender bias. He ended up almost—stress on *almost*—feeling downright sorry for any guy who ever tried to hurt any of the women he'd just trained. These women had little trouble transforming from Cute, Innocent Housewives into nose-breaking, eye-jabbing, throat-box punching machines. It was awesome.)

From a young age, men are socially inculcated in the Ways of Power. Knights slaying dragons and rescuing princesses; cops going after bad guys; firemen rushing into burning buildings; soldiers sacrificing themselves for the common good . . . we guys grow up surrounded by and acutely sensitive to endless examples of what amounts to the Proper Care and Feeding of Power.

By the time we reach middle age, we're experts on the matter. We know how it feels, acts, presents itself, and is most effectively wielded. We know the difference between true power and the infinite ways fake power tries to pretend it's real. It's a beautiful kind of knowledge to have.

Because in the end power is really just something to be used in whatever way its user deems best. And *all* power, of course, comes from God.

Yeah, power corrupts. Unless it's felt, known, used, and understood as *God's* power. Then it's . . . sheer heaven.

Some reading this book might not have even been a zygote in 1987 when Ronald Reagan was set to give a speech at the Brandenburg Gate near the Berlin Wall. Back then, just thinking about the Wall coming down was absurd. It represented everything communist. But there was a speech writer who thought President Reagan's power and popularity could culminate in a challenge to change the world. From anyone but him it would have been an insult. Howard Baker and Colin Powell advised him against it, but on that amazing day in an extraordinarily powerful way, the president challenged Secretary Gorbachev to "tear down this wall!" Now, that was a man using the power and position he had to make a difference. Two years later that wall came down, because Gorbachev responded and used *his* power to change the world.

Torn down any walls lately? Well, it is not too late. Use your power for something other than to look powerful. Nothing looks weaker or wimpier than a man who uses power to keep others at bay so that he can stay where he is—with what little he has.

HE-MAN PURE GOLD #2:
Your true understanding of, and comfort with, responsibility

In middle age, not only can we finally claim some understanding of the nature of power, but we are also able to come to terms with the whole idea of being responsible.

The bottom line is that we men very often show a distinct predilection for evading responsibility. Why, you ask? Because we are human, that's why. And it's a well-documented fact that humans hate having to do just about anything at all.

Mow your lawn and trim your hedges because it's pleasant outside work and makes your yard look great? Fun! *Have* to mow your lawn and trim your hedges, because someone from your homeowners' association came out to your place, measured your lawn and hedges, found them to be .5 centimeters too long, and you're now going to get fined?

Not fun at all.

The point is: Responsibility means obligation, and obligation *must* mean a curtailing of freedom. And taking away our freedom is bad. It's what we fought the British for, man!

Humans love freedom like fish love water. They pretty much have to have it.

Now, of course, what humans also love is having decent, clean, productive, emotionally rewarding lives. And *that* (curse that Adam and Eve!) means work. And work (curse that Adam and Eve!) means responsibility.

So there we have it: We must do what we are loath to do.

This probably explains why at one time or another we men prove to be less than entirely He-Manlike in handling our responsibilities. Constantly pulled in different directions, we often make commitments not because we value a certain idea or task but because we don't want to hurt the person who's asking. Not so good, right? Ends up creating hurt feelings, disappointed expectations, all kinds of emotional turmoil. Ends up breaking hearts.

I will never forget being introduced to the concept of responsibility. I had learned much about *ir*responsibility from my mom and dad; I knew perfectionist, black-and-white living, but I did not know what it meant to simply be responsible. That is, until I found myself miserable in just about every area of my life.

A counselor, actually my very first counselor at age twenty-eight, introduced me to *The Road Less Traveled* by M. Scott Peck. The second half of the book was a bit weird, but the first half was life changing. For the first time I saw the irresponsible rebel I had become. I cared about me and my agenda, so others just had to get used to it. I was selfish, so I was late and others had to live with it. I was lazy, so I demanded that others compensate. My success was in spite of me rather than because of me.

Reading the book, I was challenged to pick up the pieces of my life; I learned that sometimes—and especially when dealing with oneself—doing the toughest thing is often the best thing.

It was painful, but from pain grows understanding, and by middle age we (usually) have earned the right to claim real clarity on the issue of responsibility. We know what it means, what it costs, what it entails. We know how careful we should be before committing to anything more substantive than declaring the correct time to someone on the street. We understand our actions and our promises have (usually very predictable) consequences.

Words, we have learned, matter. For in the beginning was the Word, and the Word was with God, and the Word *was* God.

HE-MAN PURE GOLD #3:
Your understanding of how, little by little, mountains can be moved

One Sunday morning when John was a kid, his father told him to weed the rocks in the front yard, which he hated doing. For starters, he didn't understand why they had nothing but rocks in the little strip of land that ran between the sidewalk and the street—the area where most neighbors had grass. Worse yet, the rocks were gnarly, sharp chunks of granite that pierced a kid's hand like a pinecone rubbed into one's face.

Immediately upon hearing of that morning's chore for him, John began to do what as a kid he did best: Heavily Mope. And his father then kicked in at what *he* excelled at, which was ignoring John's moping. And so before long, John was slumped like the victim of some Greek suburban tragedy on the sidewalk in front of his house.

It was a sunny weekend morning. All his friends were playing in the park across the street. He was stuck weeding rocks. It was as wrong as wrong gets.

So John decided to take so long weeding the rocks that his father would rue the day that he tried to turn his own flesh and blood into the Cheapest Possible Manual Labor. He'd show him—and he'd show him in public, too, which he knew would drive him insane.

With maximum slowness, John reached for the first little weed and extracted it with about the same care Her Majesty's dentist might use removing one of the queen's incisors.

Fully ensconced in the drama he was creating, John accidentally finished the whole job. He had meant to go slow—he *had* gone slow—but lo and behold, when he looked back he saw nothing but weedless rocks. *Wow,* John thought. *So if you just do a little bit, and while you're doing it focus really hard, before long you've done a lot.*

We've all learned that lesson countless times over, because if there's one thing you can say about men, it's that we know how to work. Then again, we also know how to avoid as much work as possible. When we're finally ready to roll up our sleeves, though, we Guy Types want to go all out. We find it a bit challenging if patience is required. We tend to chafe at the distance between what is and what we can imagine being. But our job, as thoughtful, wanting-to-be-wise middle-aged guys, is to as much as possible make our nature like God's. And of all things, God is *the* king of Slowly But Surely.

We in our little lives can't hope to manifest a lot of divine patience, of course—but at middle age we *can* reflect upon our own times and experiences. Slowly but surely, as we have been created, we ourselves have created. *Work* has been done. On us, on everyone we know, on everything that exists.

God, of course, creates mountains. Little by little, and piece by piece, we have moved them.

Before going on, I want to cover just one other thought related to John and his early slacking and lacking as a lawn care professional. When he finally got down to the work, he did what many people do far beyond childhood. He worked in a way that he thought would punish his father. He took his time so that perhaps his father would feel pity or compassion. Rather than wanting to get the job done or do it well, the goal was to cause as much distress as possible to another person.

Surely you see the parallel of this and what others do as adults. They work, but it is in reaction to a parent to either prove how wrong or right they were. They stay stuck in a childish game, not punishing the other person but punishing themselves and never fully picking up their own lives.

HE-MAN PURE GOLD #4:
Your legitimate claim to bravery, born of almost countless challenges faced and overcome

Being brave is a tremendous quality; in a way, for us guys, it's *the* quality. But because of this high regard, most of us are hesitant to deem ourselves brave. We might think that in the past we've done something that seemed kind of brave, or we might harbor the idea that we could be brave if called upon. Still, we usually don't believe we simply *are* brave, we've always *been* brave, that next to us Batman is a regular Barney Fife.

Well, in a true way that's important, next to us Batman *is* Barney Fife, because at least Batman wears a mask whenever *he* goes out into the world. Sure, he also wears a pair of bikini briefs over a pair of tights (talk about bravely putting it all out there), but basically the guy's hiding all the time. We regular guys never get to hide from anything. Everyone always knows it's us, bravely turning in that report our boss wanted, bravely signing those mortgage papers, bravely changing those diapers.

When's the last time Batman had to go to a parent-teacher meeting about his child? When's the last time Superman bet the future of his whole family on a job he decided to take? When's the last time the Incredible Hulk took a very difficult entrance exam for . . . well . . . anything?

Superheroes. Please. Let one of *them* show up for a prostate examination. They'd be out of there quicker than you can say, "Look! Up in the sky! It's that guy who was just in the waiting room!"

All of us have faced innumerable challenges—ones we lost, won, or just survived through sheer grit and determination. Any of the three ultimately contributes to our courageousness. But we tend not to think of ourselves in those kinds of terms, because . . . well, because we're normal, humble people, and normal, humble people are not (thank goodness) prone to thinking of themselves as particularly brave. But we are particularly brave. We get out there and do stuff. We try stuff. We risk stuff. We look at what's there, and if we think it needs to be rearranged, we put our You Know What on the line and start messing with that thing. We see what happens! If it turns out great, we climb aboard and ride it to the next place it takes us. If it falls apart, we try to blame someone else, and . . . no wait, that's not what we meant to say . . . we try to figure out what went wrong, and then see if we can't make it all right again.

Of course, our legitimate claim to bravery rests a lot less on what we've done than on what we've been. We've been hurt kids, confused teens, frightened young men—and (God knows) we've been hurt, confused, and frightened grown men.

You know the great old definition of bravery—how it boils down to doing something that you've got good reason to fear doing? Well, a *lot* about regular, everyday life is intimidating—and we go through it all anyway, don't we? We don't go through the difficulties of life because we're brave; we do so because we're alive, and so have no choice in the matter beyond suicide, which is no choice at all. But a man who has survived a long climb up a high mountain has no less claim to bravery because he *had* to make that climb than does the man who climbed the same mountain simply because he chose to. Climbed is climbed. Distilled experience contributes to character. And everything that's survived brings to its survivor a measure of bravery.

Or it *should*, anyway. Make sure it does with you. Go over your life—go over your day, for that matter—and look at all the things you've either conquered or survived. Be proud of those things. Hold in your heart and mind for a moment the bravery they brought forth in you, the way you stepped up and accepted the challenge they presented. Because those things give you the right to claim for yourself that you are, in fact, courageous; you're brave; you understand what it is to make your way through something difficult you could have surely avoided had you chosen to.

If your life so far has been about you, make the second half about God. Sometimes we're shy about coming before God, because we question the completeness of our worthiness. But know this: Time and time and time again you have undoubtedly demonstrated the kind of courage that would (and someday will) make Jesus proud of you.

I am privileged to witness some of the bravest men in the world perform feats of astonishing wonder. First of all, after a lifetime of secretiveness, they show up at a weekend event called "Every Man's Battle," "Healing Is a Choice," or "Lose It for Life." They know they will be challenged to open up, confess, and change the way they are living life. With fear, trembling, resentment, anger, and stubborn resistance, they come to accept the challenges that other men are just too weak to take on. I watch them free themselves from the burdens of guilt and shame. I watch tears pour out as they feel the love and acceptance of other men. I see them connect and become men in the company of men. It is true bravery, as outstanding as any bodily feat. Each one proves that no man has to remain a coward. You, even you, can decide to risk and reap the rewards of a brave life.

HE-MAN: Movin' On

So there we have it: We He-Men of the Universe (HMUs) tend to expect much of ourselves, feel entitled, suppress our emotions, and be Solitary Men. At the same time, our life experiences have taught us all we need to know about power, responsibility, work, and what it really means to have courage.

Cool enough!

So what's next for us?

Well, another thing that's true about men is that we are by nature big fans of resolution. That's why superheroes and other Formidable Male Personages always resolve things. Superman never swoops in, exercises his super powers, saves the day, and then goes, "Well, my work here is done well enough. That one criminal got away—the guy who can instantly freeze all the water in the world—and someone will definitely need to right that tipped-over train. But other than that, I believe everything here is pretty darn adequate!"

No. Superman *catches* Mr. Ice Capades, and then he is the one who *rights* the train. He does all of this because He-Men do not enjoy raggedy edges. He knows that a raggedy edge has threads. And if you pull the right thread, everything comes unraveled and a new kind of trouble is on your hands.

As the wise man said: Things fall apart.

And as the He-Man responded: Not on my watch, they don't.

And so what, at this point in your life, can your now *seasoned and surrendered* masculinity most do for you? It can turn you into *exactly* the kind of man that you and every other man in the world have always wanted to be.

It can turn you into a man who is finally, and fully, integritous.

Wait. Integrityous.

Integritus.

Integriful?

Integrilicious?

Whoa, whoa, hold on here. Excuse us while we check a dictionary.

Um. News flash: There is, apparently, no word in the English language for "full of integrity."

A guy boasts a lot; he's boastful. Can't decide stuff; he's indecisive. Full of honesty; he's honest. Filled with deceit; he's deceitful. All that makes sense, right?

Well, as it turns out, if someone is full of integrity, about *all* you can say about them is that they're . . . full of integrity. Still, in the secret, universal Language of God, we're sure there's a word for "defined by integrity," and that God is definitely pleased by people who exemplify integrity.

Hmmm. Christian men being told they should be men of integrity. Gee, it's not like any of us have ever heard *that* before, is it?

Sigh.

Then again, the word *integrity* is like Google: It gets used a lot because it works. There *is* no word like integrity; it's one of those words—like lasagna, foot, suffocate, pantomime, boneless, and so on—for which only that word will do. So, overused or not, *integrity* does the trick.

Let us, then, at least make sure that we're perfectly clear on what the word means.

Back to the dictionary! And here's how the fourth edition of *The American Heritage Dictionary* defines *integrity:* "Steadfast adherence to a strict moral or ethical code."

And boom. There it is.

A steadfast adherence to a moral or ethical code. That's it. That's what makes a man a man; *that's* the difference between a boy and a man. A boy can certainly be aware of a strict moral or ethical code, but it takes a real man to steadfastly adhere to the same.

And such a man would be none other than you.

You, with all your scars, pains, modified hopes, and dreams long ago abandoned. You, who have learned the harm of expecting too much of yourself, of taking what you have for granted, of suppressing your emotions, of insisting that you can handle everything yourself. You, the expert on power, responsibility, work, courage.

Age and experience teach us that life isn't about absolutes; rather than blacks and whites, it's mostly about grays. You know how to wait for a thing to reveal to you its true nature; how to listen to people and environments tell you what they are, what they want, and of what exactly they're composed. You know how to appraise opportunities and situations that a younger man would simply jump right into because they looked so tempting and gratifying.

And there's a world of wisdom in that, isn't there?

At this point in your life, the world belongs to you. Within you is the strength and wisdom to let go of the worldly things and steadfastly adhere to the magnificent things:

Your God.

Your knowledge of what's right and wrong.

The people you love.

The commitments you make.

The promises you extend.

The moral structure you determine is worthy of your fidelity.

The integrity to which you have a rightful claim.

That's what middle age is for, so that you can finally own and become the *real* He-Man that you've always dreamed of being.

Middle age isn't about being weakened or confused or getting used to your limitations or any of that nonsense. Middle age is about earning the right to finally understand what it really means to say that you are made in God's image. And if God isn't the *ultimate* He-Man of the Universe, then . . . then he doesn't exist at all.

But he does.

And he is.

And you definitely are.

If you are like us, there are times when you just want to be told what to do and then you will do it. Here are some things you can do to be a better man.

HE-MAN: Things to Do

1. Spend time thinking about how you got your ideas about what men are supposed to be, how they are supposed to act and feel. Write down the qualities that you learned men should have or believe they should have. Then consider your relationship to each one of those qualities. What do you think? Has possessing—or desiring—the Classical Manly Qualities (assuming the CMQs are what ended up on your list) worked for you in your life? Have they hurt you? Inspired you? Threatened you? To what extent do you think you own them, and to what extent do they own you? What role do you think they might be playing in whatever you're going through these days? In what ways, if any, do you think the CMQs have impacted your relationship with God?

2. List three men in your personal life who have meant the most to you. Then list the characteristics about each of those men that you feel makes them so admirable. Ask yourself what the relationship is between the very real qualities these men possess and the sort of abstract qualities that our culture tells us Real Men ought to possess. In what ways do or don't they jibe?

3. During, say, half of one of the days that you're operating out in the world, try to be aware of how (if at all) the simple fact of being a man helps you in life. What confidences does it

give you, for instance? What positive assumptions are made about you because you're a man? Any? *Is* it a man's world, do you think? If so, how do you think you might (however consciously or unconsciously) take advantage of that fact?

4. Conversely, monitor your experiences out in the world with an eye toward discerning in what ways being a man *isn't* such a great thing. What expectations are put upon you—to, say, constantly assert yourself, or to always be in control? How do those expectations affect the quality of your experiences? Do you think sometimes you might actually prefer to be a woman or a little kid? Why or why not?

5. Make a list of those qualities that you think of as primarily male in nature that may at times have interfered with your relationship with God. Go down that list, and about each quality have a prayerful conversation with God. Just present those qualities or characteristics to him, and see what, in response, he puts into your heart about each one.

6. Think about something or someone in your life right now (including anything about yourself or your own behavior) that is not how you'd like it—something that regularly causes you stress or psychological discomfort. Now ask yourself: "Is it possible that the reason [so-and-so] bothers me so much is because it so clashes with my idea of what [so-and-so] should be?" Depending on your answer, make a list of the qualities that you'd like [so-and-so] to possess or exhibit.

Then make a separate list of the qualities that [so-and-so] *does* possess or exhibit. Now spend some time with those two lists. What, if any, differences do you see between them? Are any qualities in the two lists mutually exclusive? If so, which of the two qualities do you think will ultimately win out: your idea of what [so-and-so] should be, or the reality of what [so-and-so] is? Is there anything you can or should do to change the reality of [so-and-so], so that it more closely resembles your idea of what (or who) it should be? What will that effort cost you? What impact will it have on the nature of [so-and-so]? Finally, consider whether, in the end, it would be worth the cost of whatever it would take you to change [so-and-so] to whatever you want it to be. If it would be, then it looks like you've got some work to do. If it *wouldn't* be worth it, then it looks like you just relieved yourself of a lot of stress.

SON | 3

FROM THE FIRST moment we're squeezed out of the real Happiest Place on Earth (far happier than Disneyland) to the first moment that God welcomes us into the Very Best Place Ever, we remain, forever and always, someone's son.

Look in the mirror, and what do you see? Some of your father, some of your mother. Some of their mother and father, too. And a little of *their* ma and pa. And (you can bet) a little of *their* parents.

What you see, flickering behind the face and eyes of the person in the mirror, is countless eons of time and history. Maybe someone who fought alongside the Vikings. Maybe someone who during the Renaissance wasn't sure they liked all that new highfalutin art. Maybe someone who rode an animal that's now extinct. Maybe a man who once held a spear or bow outside his family's dwelling in the dead of night, listening for enemies.

All of those dreams, despairs, hopes, challenges, loves, lives, and deaths in your particular branch of the Family of Man eventually came down, very specifically, to you. You! The son of people *born* of people! Who were born of people! Who were born of people! Who were . . . well, you get the idea.

There's a lot going on when you look in the mirror, isn't there? Lots of lives in there. Lots of identities. Lots of history. And while you can hardly fathom it all, you sure are familiar with what it's resulted in.

What's weird—well, *one* of the things that's weird—about being human is how long we spend utterly dependent upon our parents. Like, *years*. As we (your authors) understand it, that's actually quite rare in the animal kingdom. It's usually just, like, "Tra-la-la, tra-la-la, I'm a pregnant animal of the wild, frolicking around my environment, and—whoa, something's coming out of me! Why, it's a baby! What a cutie! Okay, Junior, up and at 'em! Childhood's over! Why, just look at you run! And good thing, too, 'cuz out here, you either run quick or die quick! Go on, now! Good-bye! Good luck surviving!"

That sure isn't how it works for us humans, is it? My wife, Misty, and I had sex one night, and nine months later a cartoon character came out of her while my daughter Madeline and I looked on in horror and wonder. It was quite the bonding experience. That was Solomon Russell Arterburn, who at the time of this writing is eleven months old. So far, he can say "ball," "bird," "Oprah," "cookie," "Ma-Ma," and "Da-Da." He can also yell louder than any of us when he needs something. Most cannot understand what he is yelling, but I can. Translated, it goes like this: "Hey, servants! I need your full and undivided attention in here. I have undergone over thirty seconds of terror being alone or wet or dirty or hungry. I don't care what else you are doing. Drop it and run. Now, get moving!"

And we just think that is the cutest thing in the world for him to be so demanding. We love it that he even knows he needs something. And we love it that when we focus on him, it calms him down. Sadly, I have known men who were just like that when they were forty. If all the attention was not on them or someone was not trying to meet their every need, their lives were very miserable.

One man came for help who had achieved that most miserable state of learned helplessness. No job was good enough to keep and no person comfortable enough to connect with. Nothing worked because he could work nothing. And it all made perfect sense when you heard about how his "loving" mother treated him when he was younger. He did not learn to walk until he was three. Not because he was developmentally handicapped, but because whenever he cried, he stayed put until his mother picked him up. And she always picked him up. Those first few years he lived as a totally helpless baby. Sad but true. So the helpless baby became the helpless man.

The extreme is easy to see. For perspective on our own situations we can benefit from backing away from the extreme and considering where we fall on the continuum of competence and helplessness. Like this man, there may be distinct factors for our present lot in life, but it is our responsibility to fix it, no matter how it developed.

The way it is supposed to work is that when we show up, looking like miniature Fred Mertzes (of *I Love Lucy* fame) and screaming our lungs out, we're about as helpless as helpless gets—and we stay helpless for a long time. Thoughtless burp machines though we may seem to be, we are collecting and processing massive amounts of information about who we are and what we're supposed to do and be. And we acquire and absorb most of that knowledge from Mom and Dad.

Who acquired it from their mom and dad.

Who acquired it from their mom and dad.

Who acquired it from their mom and dad.

Until someone, way, way back, acquired it from Adam and/or Eve—who, as we all know all too well, are really at the . . . um . . . core of most of our problems today.

People, their parents, and the grief and joy thereof.

It's a story as old as . . . well, us.

SON GOOD RIDDANCE #1:
Being physically dependent

One of the greatest things about "growing up" is no longer having to rely upon your parents for your emotional and/or physical well-being. When you're a kid, what choice do you have in . . . well, any matter at all? As a baby, if you want to go somewhere, you have to wait for someone to *carry* you there. Terrible! And if you get hungry, there's no way you can just order in a pizza. Instead, you just have to hope someone notices you're hungry and feeds you. Again, less than ideal.

SON GOOD RIDDANCE #2:
The assumption that your knowledge and/or understanding is insufficient

The idea that because you're a kid nothing you think is valid is one of the worst things about childhood. While it's never really been clear why it should be assumed that a taller, hairier human is necessarily smarter than a shorter, smoother one, this prejudice persists. Though children the world over continue to rail against this deeply ingrained societal injustice, nobody listens to them because they're just kids and are always going on about one thing or another.

SON GOOD RIDDANCE #3:
Being emotionally dependent

As a kid your parents pretty much dominate your emotional landscape. They're upset; you're upset. They're happy; you're happy. They're angry; you're scared. As children, basically all we do is respond emotionally to our parents. We're like little emotional slaves to their outsized emotional states.

And then we grow older, and existing as a primarily dependent and reactive human being isn't necessary anymore. We get to be happy whenever we want to be happy, mad whenever we want to be mad, and upset when we want to be upset.

Finally, we're the captain of our ship!

What do we usually tend to find, though? Most of us along the line realize that we get happy, mad, and upset at the same things that made our parents happy, mad, and upset.

Life! It's such a mystery!

Or not.

SON GOOD RIDDANCE #4:
The things your parents taught you about life that were just plain wrong

Man, this issue and the next (the things your parents taught you about *you* that were just plain wrong) are definitely the two big "gifts" of childhood that just keep on . . . taking. They sure are for lots of us, anyway. It again gets back to the fact that most of us were raised by people who were . . . well, people. And most people have all kinds of stuff rattling around inside their brains and hearts that doesn't entirely mesh with the greater, truer reality. As it happens, people are also pretty fond of sex and/or procreation, which means that sooner or later, most of them have children. And naturally, as parents those people communicate to their children *all* of their ideas and attitudes about the world—the positive and negative.

Children, being the perceptive Absorbo Machines that they are, thoroughly internalize that information and slowly but surely (and usually not all that slowly) come to incorporate those thoughts and feelings into their own worldview. It simply can't be helped. Even if as children we had possessed anywhere near the cognitive faculties to evaluate our parents' thoughts and feelings, our love for them would have kept us from doing so *too* critically.

When we're kids, about the only thing we know is that we unconditionally love our parents. And we sure depend on them to teach us everything about ourselves and the world. If our dad tells us that as caterpillars become butterflies so do worms become hummingbirds, then we're going to think it's only a matter of time before any worm flies. And if our mom tells us that, say, failing to eat all the food on our dinner plate every night is a sin, then it's likely to be pretty hard for us to avoid becoming overweight.

As kids we just *believe* our parents. We believe in what they do. We believe in what they say. We believe in what they *are*. Period.

And that's a beautiful thing.

But every so often it can also become a troubling thing. As often happens, we adults come to realize that the whole "Life 1.0" program that was downloaded and integrated into our own operating system via MomandDad.net contains a few bugs. And at some point along our life path, some of us discover that those bugs have evolved into viruses strong enough to . . . well, cause us to crash sometimes.

The problem, of course, is that it can be very difficult for us to find, isolate, and delete whatever bugs or viruses we inherited via our familial shareware. The stuff that as babies and kids we learn from our parents sinks into us low and deep. We *own* what we get from our parents. It's ours. We believe it like we thought of it. And in a way—either as a reaction to the original input or because of the way we just naturally incorporate it into our own lives—we usually do turn the Dysfunctional Stuff that we inherit from our parents into something uniquely our own.

Take, for instance, a friend of Steve's, a man whom we'll call Randall. Randall's father was an exceptionally angry man. He wasn't physically violent—he never struck his wife, kids, or anyone else—but his mood and attitude were always almost harrowingly intense. Incongruously enough, Randall's dad was also a very successful salesman. A tall, athletic, handsome man, he possessed a booming voice and an extremely quick (if decidedly sarcastic) wit. He could actually be a pretty fun guy to hang out with.

Except when he was home. Then, not so much. In the confines of his house, Randall's father seemed to always be extremely angry at someone or something: the "idiot" at work who couldn't process orders right; the "moron" of a customer who just couldn't grasp how to place an order; the "[bleepin'] [bleepin']" truck driver who arrived at the customer's too late to make a delivery.

No matter the time or place, Randall's dad was always fuming about something. The poor guy had three heart attacks by the time he was fifty; his first dropped him when he was only thirty-nine. And each heart attack seemed to make him madder about the world in general.

As for Randall, when he was about thirty-five, do you know what problem he finally felt he needed to face and resolve? That he was afraid of life. He hadn't grown up to be angry like his father. No, he had grown up feeling afraid that life must be bad for his father to react to it as venomously as he usually did.

Through therapy, reflection, and prayer, what Randall came to realize is that his father wasn't an angry man. His father was a *terrified* man. He raged about everything because he found everything threatening. It was his father's fear that Randall picked up on and internalized as a kid; he "learned" from his father that life and people are designed to hurt you, that they have the power to suck the very joy of life out of you. So whereas his father channeled his fear into an aggression that allowed him to get out there and dominate people and situations, Randall grew into someone who tended to shy away from the world, out of an assumed distrust and fear of it.

Randall had seen the damage the world could really do. His father had shown him how destructive and caustic a place it really was.

If, like his father, Randall had been constantly angry, it would have been easier for him to know and name his problem. But as it was, for a long time and without consciously being aware of it, Randall simply assumed that life was inherently threatening. He accepted that as "fact," a core truth about life.

Well, that's *not* life, is it? Randall was wrong about that. Just as his father before him had been wrong about that.

You can imagine Randall's joy as he began to realize that life wasn't what he assumed it to be. He'd always just thought he had some sort of nervous disorder. Thank God for his mercy and for Randall's determination to live a life that was happier than he'd ever known.

In order to increase his understanding of himself and life, and to thereby simply enjoy life more, Randall took the time and the effort necessary to unlearn something wrong about life that his father had taught him.

Most of us would benefit from the same thing, to look deep and hard at our own emotional legacies—to the basic assumptions about life we inherited from our parents. Like Randall, we, too, might have a thing or two inside of ourselves that we'd do well to unlearn.

SON GOOD RIDDANCE #5:
The things that your parents taught you about *you* that were just plain wrong

Yikes. This is the Truly Hairy one; the life-issue that keeps shrinks, pastors, priests, cops, and pharmacists in business. And this, of course, is the one that causes too many of us to spend too many nights lying awake, wondering what is wrong with us.

What's *really* wrong with us, of course, is that we belong to a fallen race; and to remedy that tragedy we have the glory of Christ. Beyond that there's rarely anything intrinsically wrong with any of us—with the exception of one tiny detail: some/many/most (you be the judge!) of us had parents who weren't exactly graduates of Ideal Parents U. Which means that as kids a lot of us absorbed and learned things *about ourselves* that later proved to be less than helpful to becoming the kind of men we always wanted to be.

Here's the usual formula: As kids we learn from our parents some wrong stuff about ourselves; we then incorporate that stuff into our concept of who we are. When we go out into the world, we jam up in certain areas of our emotional and/or psychological lives. We find we can't do much about those difficult areas of our lives (insofar as we find that trying to change our personality or automatic responses to certain kinds of people, situations, or environments feels like trying to control what our livers or gallbladders do). Finally, we keep plugging away at life anyway, because what other choice do we really have?

And there it is. For most of us, that's pretty much How Life Goes.

At least until now. Because now we're middle-aged. And middle age, thank God, is where all that begins to change. At this point in our lives, we've been around Ye Olde Block so many times that it's reasonable for us to expect and/or downright insist that any holes in our lives—certainly any big holes—get filled.

We want a smoother ride now. We're ready to have our lives be better, easier, richer, nicer, and generally more fulfilling than ever before.

The first potholes that have been bouncing us around and need to be filled are whatever destructive, shame-producing things that we as children learned about ourselves from our parents.

And let's be clear about this: It's not our purpose here to blame our parents for whatever esteem-dinting "lessons" they may have taught us. Nobody's perfect. We all know that. Everyone's got stuff that they trip about, for reasons that are perfectly understandable. So this is not about assigning blame. But it is about fact. And the fact is that just by nature of the parent-child relationship, a fair number of us *did* pick up bad information about ourselves that can pull us down. But being middle-aged means we finally have a right to once and for all get rid of all that dead weight.

It must be said, however, that divesting ourselves of unhealthy things we learned about ourselves from our parents is decidedly difficult. Rejecting what our parents believed—especially rejecting whatever they apparently believed about us—cannot help but feel to us exactly like rejecting our parents. The reason this is true is because when you love someone, you love their mind. A person's mind is who they are. So if you reject someone's mind, you pretty much reject their entire being. And for most of us, rejecting our parents at that kind of level instinctively feels like we're waving good-bye to them as they drift out to the sea on the ice floe we've forced them onto.

Not a good feeling. An unthinkably awful one, actually. Better to sacrifice ourselves than to sacrifice our parents, whom we tend to love more than we do ourselves.

All of which boils down to this: Most of us, by instinct and nature, would rather spend our lives with our backs bent, carrying our parents, than stand up straight and let our parents fall to the ground.

So there we are. Stuck with some "gifts" from our parents that we sure don't want, but lacking the fundamental emotional resources to return them. What to do?

Well, like all challenges that are basically too complex or personally challenging for us to handle on our own, this is where God comes in.

The great Lord Almighty is our true parent—it is, after all, he who gave us life and keeps us alive still. And in his infinite wisdom and compassion, the Lord saw fit to give us the very parents that he did. If that resulted in more challenges than we prefer, we can trust that God structured our lives exactly as he did for reasons too wondrous for us to even begin knowing this side of eternity. And while on this earth, what we *can* do is take the time, and do the emotional work necessary, to identify those perceptions and ideas about ourselves that are not only *not* natural to us, but that in fact work contrary to God's love for us.

Once we're cognizant of the Bad Messages forever playing in our heads about ourselves, we have what amounts to a moral obligation to hold our parents responsible for creating, fueling, and harnessing us with those messages. We *have* to write

"Return to Sender" on that misdelivered package and send it back. This is exactly where most of us stop on the road to healing. We don't want to deal with the idea that our parents hurt us emotionally. We don't want to release our deep-seated need to have our parents be, in effect, wonderful, well-meaning people who would never do or mean us any harm.

We'd rather wear the itchy, too-small shirt our parents made for us than risk hurting them by giving it back to them.

But here's the thing: We can take off that uncomfortable shirt and not return it. We don't have to yell at or confront our parents for in effect insisting that we wear that awful shirt. We can confront them, of course—but we don't have to. We just have to allow ourselves the full, rich knowledge that our parents passed some stuff to us that had everything to do with the flawed, fallen people they were and nothing to do with the innocent, loving children we were.

We just have to heal. *That's* the whole of our obligation. And there's nothing fearful in that. We have nothing to fear from holding our parents responsible for what is their responsibility; our parents have nothing to fear from our apprehending the truth of how we were raised. Spiritual and psychological healing is always a beautiful thing. If you know the details of your healing would hurt your parents, then spare them those details. If you think it might help them to hear about how you were healed, then share it with them. Who knows? Maybe your story will help them heal from their parents. Maybe they'll feel blessed and relieved that you've finally brought out onto the table something that's long been anguishing them.

The main thing to know—the reason it's *always* safe to heal—is because healing means letting go. Once you've divested yourself of whatever baggage got strapped onto you as a kid, you feel truly and deeply relieved. A relieved person isn't angry. A relieved person is grateful.

And a relieved Christian, of course, is grateful to God.

And God and resentment never exist in the same place.

But God and love? God and forgiveness?

That's how, in fact, people can go home again.

SON PURE GOLD #1:
The utter, instinctive joy of being a kid

When John was a kid, he lived across the street from an apricot orchard that was about two miles square.

Many trees!

Many apricots!

Better than Disneyland!

So he and his fellow suburbanite pals used to practically live in this orchard. They had the dirt, the dirt clods, the shade, the food hanging right off the trees, the dappled sun, the perfect place to hide from Larger People they wanted to avoid.

As you can imagine, that orchard was the scene of epic apricot fights. One time, precisely as he was dodging his way behind a tree, John nailed his best friend Stanley Queen in the middle of his back with an apricot so ripe it was like hitting him with a water balloon filled with jam.

In slow-motion fashion, Stanley Queen went from frantically running, to being struck, to throwing his head back, to arching his back, to throwing his arms up and out, to moving downward, to collapsing into the dirt pained, stained, and laughing.

And at that moment John—still in the full-bodied extension in which he'd released his Apricot to End All Apricots—thought exactly this: *This is perfect. The absolute perfect Ten-Year-Old-Boy Moment. I will never, ever forget seeing Stanley Queen, whom I love like the brother I never had, go down like a hysterical wounded maniac behind a tree that, tragically, he reached all too late.*

That moment stamped itself on John's mind and heart so vividly that he can recall it years later exactly as he had enjoyed it way back then. And in his memory he's got . . . what? . . . *hundreds* of other such Perfect Childhood Moments.

And so do you.

And that's an exquisitely good thing, isn't it?

Jobs. Briefcases. Neckties. Making sure the margins and borders of the report we've got to turn in Monday morning are all lined up just right.

Okay. That's all fine and necessary and good.

But in a lot of ways we all understand, it's as boys that we were really the best men we'd ever be, wasn't it?

SON PURE GOLD #2:
Every life lesson we learned as boys

It's a strange fact about life that just about anything we really need to know we learn by the time we're about eight. And *that's* pushing it: One of the reasons the book *All I Really Need to Know I Learned in Kindergarten* sold so many copies was because everyone just naturally agreed with its title.

Play fair. Be nice. Do your work. Take responsibility for what you do. Don't try to whistle with your mouth full. Practice makes perfect. Pet cats in only one direction. Lying is dishonorable. Sometimes we learn life basics via an adult who cares enough to make sure we grasp whatever concept is at hand; sometimes we learn through observing others; sometimes it's just the ol' Elementary School of Hard Knocks. Who knows how or where we learned everything we did? But as boys we learned a lot about life, and every day since then we've built upon that invaluable body of knowledge.

What's true when you're six, is true when you're ten, is true when you're twenty, is true when you're sixty. It might be time to sit down with a blank sheet of paper and try to recall the things you learned before you were eight.

Here's to those who helped us get it right when we were six.

SON PURE GOLD #3:
The emotional wherewithal it took to survive childhood

Being a kid is tough. Richie Rich, John-Boy Walton, Super Boy, it doesn't matter: If you're a kid, you spend a lot of time getting Seriously Harassed, if not outright pounded into the dirt, by that oversized bully-to-end-all-bullies that is General Life. As adults, we sometimes forget how true that is for kids; we tend to think that, like those they're afflicting, the problems of children are small. But as Einstein showed us, everything is relative, and a kid who's gotten himself ostracized from his social group surely suffers no less than the grown man who has, say, gotten himself fired from his job. Each feels his loss like a bullet to the chest.

Except the man has something going for him not available to the boy: Experience.

Experience! It's where perspective comes from, and kids don't have much of it at all. That's why everything bad that happens feels to them like the end of the world.

And then—surprise!—they find that it isn't. They manage. They reconstruct their ideas about reality. They plunge into behavior they hope produces the results they desire—and if it doesn't, they recoup, lick their wounds, and try another tack.

Children survive.

They survive because they're full of life, and what God means to grow continues to grow.

I have known men who had been sexually abused by their father all through childhood. I know one man who was deeply loved one night and beaten by his drunken dad the next. He trembled in fear wondering which Dad would come home. For me abuse did not come from a parent. It came from my older brother Jerry. He would beat me with a tennis racquet and ridicule me mercilessly. I did not know he was acting out his own frustration on me. He had been molested and told no one, and the older he got the more of an impact it had on him. I was the easy target and I lived in fear, until he shoved me one day, and I shoved him back into the fireplace. He never touched me again, but the damage was done. I would for years feel inadequate and afraid of other males. This was not sibling rivalry, it was sibling abuse. Survive I did, but not without a few scars.

Survival is no small feat for any of us. But it should for the rest of our lives provide some seriously dependable support and encouragement.

SON PURE GOLD #4:
The enduring, deeply affective nature of family

One thing you can't really appreciate until you're older is the impact your family has on your personality and entire life. When you're a kid, the people in your family are such an integral part that you can't even imagine what reality would be like without your particular dad, your particular mom, or your particular brother or sister. All you know is that you have the family that you do, and . . . that's that. You adjust to them, you respond to them, you do or don't enjoy certain things about them—but mostly, you just kind of go around them.

Then you get older, and you really go your own way: You venture out into the world, impress who you are against that world, and see what results.

And then you get older still. And what you're finally in a position to do—right around middle age, as it happens—is to look back and understand how deeply you were affected by your family. You are always your father's son; you are always your mother's boy. Love your family; hate your family; have mixed feelings about each member of your family—however you feel about them, you realize how *much* of who you are is determined by the family you were born into.

You can divorce your wife. You can even turn your back on God. But you're fully connected to your family for every single second of your life. Your cells are theirs. Your body is theirs. Your blood is theirs.

Sound like a familiar dynamic at all?

To some degree that's as real as spilt blood; your family sacrificed itself for you—just as you sacrificed yourself for it. The entire give-and-take relationship between us and our families is just one of the ways that God prepares our spirits to come and be with the family into which all we Christians were born, and to which (yay!) we will all soon enough return.

Our families are models for our coming—and, in fact, for our present—life with God. Everything we need to know, one way or another, is there.

SON: Movin' On

So let's go out on a limb and dare to venture that you, Reader Man, feel whatever you feel about your childhood with a great deal of intensity. And do you know why we know that's true? Because you're human, that's why. And every human looks back on his or her childhood with that kind of powerfully nostalgic Intenso-Vibe that we will forgo trying to describe since we know you already know what we're talking about.

We know that when you start anything you say with "When I was a kid . . ." you're about to say something that really matters to you. We know that about the *only* way to make you cry is to get you to remember something that meant a lot to you as a kid.

Why is that, do you think? Why do you think we all tend to feel such strong emotions about our childhoods?

Our answer to that is because there's an ever-compelling purity to the state of childhood. When we are kids—from toddlers to, say, eight years old—we barely know anything about anything beyond ourselves. As children, we're entirely Pre-Persona.

Which is to say that when we are children, we exist as our authentic selves.

And then of course what happens is that we gradually become more familiar with the system around us. Slowly but surely, things and people begin to make sense. Discernible and then predictable life patterns begin to emerge. We start to realize that we're separate from everything around us. The whole Cause and Effect phenomenon starts becoming clear to us. We learn what behaviors prompt what responses. We start to take control of our lives.

In short, we begin to understand and exercise our will. And we begin exercising that will in reaction to whatever challenges are before us. We learn to do, say, and be whatever we must to most effectively and happily survive or thrive in the environment in which we're raised. And that's as good and natural a process as we have in our world; it's the healthy, inevitable means by which babies become teens and teens become adults.

But that growth—that relatively long and steady transformation—comes at an exceptionally deep cost: our inexorable, resolute abandonment of our authentic boyhood selves.

The fact is that each of us leaves behind the boy we were in order to become the "grown-up" that, after all, we must.

As boys, we may have passionately loved lizards, rocks, marionettes, running around outside in the rain—all that kind of kid stuff. But as we grew older we learned to stop being so enthusiastic about those sorts of "childish" things (or to at the very least stop showing enthusiasm for them), and to instead start acting more "mature."

And then we hit puberty—and man, puberty is *death* for All Things Little Kid-like. No more water-balloon fights. No more building hidden forts. No more staging major, fate-determining offenses and defenses with little plastic army men. All of that stuff, gone like last year's dinosaur pajamas.

Because the world is coming! *Reality* is happening! And the world and reality demand certain things of a boy meaning to become a man! Seriousness! Effort! Determination! Being tough! Getting the job done! Keeping a stiff upper lip!

Being a *man* about things!

And so—being good guys who really do just want to get along in life—we toe the line. We fall in step. We get busy at least trying to act like the man that we someday hope to actually be mistaken for.

Daily shaving, here we come!

Everything about this progression is natural, healthy, and even a lot of fun. But it does mean leaving behind that little kid wearing the cowboy hat and the satisfyingly realistic six-gun rig.

For some of us, growing up means not only willfully leaving behind the boy we were, but something much worse. It can mean in essence *betraying* that boy by slowly but surely turning ourselves into whoever our parents tell us that we are, or should be. As children, we naturally fulfill our parents' prophesies for us; we are the wax they pour into the mold of their own design. If you have parents who are psychologically and spiritually healthy, then they won't want anything different for you than what's naturally good for you.

But if you're born to parents who are uncomfortable with who they are, it's likely they're going to have some kind of agenda for you. And as a kid you're going to want to fulfill that agenda, because, crazy or not, your parents are still your parents, and you love them. A kid living in a situation like that almost can't help but get caught up in a very difficult cycle, one that can end up haunting him long after he's "grown up" and on his own.

As an example, I (Steve here) have a friend named David whose father was forever telling him that he was dumb. Now, you can say a lot of things about David, but the one thing no one who knows him *ever* says about him is that he's dumb. But his father used to constantly say or imply to David that he was a dolt; his favorite nickname for David was "knucklehead." And so David came to believe that that's who he really was; as a child, it never even occurred to him that he might be smart. And being dumb "worked" for young David, too. If he built a model airplane perfectly, his father would sneer at it and ask David who had really done the work, or act like it was a miracle that David had built the thing correctly—or he'd say how any idiot could follow directions and glue things together. But if David showed his father a model plane with the wings half hanging off and decals slapped across its windshield instead of its side, then his father would smile at him, pat him on the back, and say, "Well, boy, you did the best you could with what you've got." He maybe would tell David a story about the cool model planes that he used to build as a kid or even help David on the next airplane!

And thus was David emotionally rewarded for being slow-witted. In order for him to get that love from his father, he "only" had to betray and abandon the smart little kid he really was—the kid who collected and categorized rocks; who pored over books about life in colonial America; who, via books from the local library, learned to tell from their dress alone which areas of the country different Native North Americans were from. *That* kid wasn't getting what David wanted most in the world, which was his father's love.

Starving people do anything for food—and to a kid, a parent's love *is* like food. We all do what we must to get and keep it. Hopefully, for that love we're not asked to do or be anything unnatural or unhealthy. Most of us are too young at the time to even consider the source of our parents' love. And we don't care, either. All we know, and all we care about, is whether or not we are getting that love.

And if we're not, we'll do whatever we can to get as much of it as we can.

Before finally coming into his own as an adult, David struggled mightily with persistent low self-esteem. The low self-esteem—and resultant guilt—wasn't so much from thinking he was stupid. It came from a conviction just beneath his conscious awareness that he was despicable for essentially siding with his father against the good, smart little boy who was his true, authentic self.

Today, you'll be happy to know that David, who became a Christian, is a deeply respected author and a professor of early American history at one of our nation's top universities. Once he was out amongst it, the *world* taught David how deeply mistaken his father had been about him, praise the Lord. It's amazing what some good counseling and one-on-one with the Lord can do for a person.

So here's what we've been leading to: It would seriously behoove us middle-aged men who are looking to our futures to realize how critical it is that we look to our past, and there discern the degree to which we did the same thing as David the little boy. And what's so important to understand is that even if we didn't have parents who acted like David's dad—that is, parents who essentially forced us to betray the boy who was our authentic self—we *still* had to abandon our original boyhood self in order to finally create for ourselves a more grown-up persona.

We all had to become whoever we needed to in order to survive. It can, after all, be a pretty cruel world. And that means we all, once upon a time, left the best of ourselves behind—which, again, is entirely natural and healthy. It's something we had to do in order to become men. No one wants to see an executive at a top-level business meeting sucking his thumb or cuddling his blankie.

Life does demand that we mature.

And here's the good news: We did. We matured. We became men.

And at this point in our lives, we would do very well being open to the wonderful, liberating news that we're now free to go back and *again be with* that inner little boy whom we left behind all those many years ago.

That cowboy.

That knight in shining armor.

That brave Indian warrior.

That intrepid explorer.

That boy raised by apes who could swing on vines like lesser men *wish* they could run on the street.

That unadulterated *hero!*

Remember that kid?

Well, he sure remembers you. And if you believe nothing else in this world, believe that the little boy you used to be would welcome you back the exact same way you'd welcome your father coming to hug you until you can barely catch your breath. That boy wants you back. He understands why you did what you did. He supports you going out and making your way in the world. He knows that you went out there and did what he knows he was certainly *not* prepared to do.

Here's the deal that's as real as it gets: You are the hero of your (if you're drinking or eating, wait until you've swallowed) inner child.

Hey, man. No one said psychological health was pretty. Do you think we *like* dragging out pop-psychology terms like "inner child"? A lot of people think we ought to spank our inner child and forget about him. Lock him up and throw away the key. Well, we don't! But there it is! We're men! We do what we have to do! And if we're trying to become the best men we can be, then one of the things we have to do is come to terms with our . . . interior young'un!

Why? Because you went out there, and you really *did* slay the big, bad dragons of the world. You went to high school. You learned to drive. You got a job.

You actually kissed girls!

The reason it's so fantastic to be a middle-aged guy with the sense to obey his nagging instinct to go back and fully reclaim his inner child lies in the truth that, just like an adult can do things a kid can't, a kid can do things an adult can't. Men can serve on a jury, order a glass of wine, shave, tie a tie, care about quarterly reports.

But none of that stuff even comes *close* to what a boy can do that a "man" can't. And that (in a nutshell) is to be open. To be spontaneous. To be unselfconsciously "immature."

To forget who he is supposed to be, and to simply—gloriously—be who he is.

To push his face so far into a bowl of ice cream his nose goes numb.

To chase a butterfly all over a meadow.

To skip a rock so perfectly it practically ends up beaning someone in China.

The truth is, as men we just about never have the fun we had when we were kids, do we?

And if you really boiled down the fun that we used to have as kids to a single definition, it's that everything, in a way unique to itself, is sacred.

When you're a kid, everything is special. Everything is new. Everything is worthy of Utmost Attention.

You know what we are as kids? Open. Open and spontaneous.

As boys, most of us had no idea who we were "supposed" to be. We weren't filtering our experience through the construct of who and how we "should" be. We were just being . . . who we were. We were being our natural selves.

And now, as men, we have the opportunity to go back and again inhabit the mindset that we had as kids. We *should* learn to at times be that kid again—to sometimes let him come forward and inhabit the body and life that we now call our own. Why not? Our inner little boys are smart. They get it. His instincts, for instance, are impeccable. Someone lies to that kid, he knows it, right away. Something about a situation just doesn't feel right, and all kinds of alarms go off in his head.

Middle age is *the* time for us to reclaim our inner child. Doing so both heals our past and allows us to move into our future equipped with exactly the kind of open, trusting, spontaneous sensibility that marked our lives as kids and that is too easily left behind as adults.

Go on, man. Go back and find that little kid inside of you. Using your inner eye, see if he isn't maybe sitting on the edge of his bed back in the bedroom you grew up in. See if he's not in there, with his baseball cap on, holding his mitt in his lap, waiting for you. Wherever he is, go find him—and then give him a big ol' hug. Tell him you love him. Apologize for leaving him back where you did. Explain to him why you had to leave him back there.

He'll understand. He'll forgive you. He'll hug you back, with all of his might.

And then you guys can go get a hot dog, and then maybe go see that new animated movie that looks so unbelievably excellent.

SON: Things to Do

1. Write a letter to your father, in which you're very clear about all the ways that he disappointed and hurt you over the years. (It's helpful to do this even if your father is no longer alive or part of your life.) Give yourself permission to be brutally honest; spare the man nothing. Make the letter as long as it has to be in order for you to once and for all fully articulate your resentments. Once you've finished the letter, show it to your wife or best friend or someone very close to you. Ask them to listen to you while you talk about the letter's content. See if you don't come out of the whole experience with a different, expanded understanding of what exactly it means to be your father's son. Once you're done writing and talking about the letter, fold it up and put it away somewhere safe. There's no need to mail it; this isn't about engaging so much as it is exploring.

2. Write a letter to your father in which you tell him how much you love him and why. Talk about all the good, healthy things you learned from him, about all the positive ways in which being his son has continued to affect your life. Be honest, clear, and generous in your statements about him, as both a father and a man. This letter you *can* mail to your dad. Who wouldn't love to get a letter like that? (If your dad's passed away, consider reading it to someone close to you, especially if that person also knew or was close to your dad.)

3. In what ways, if any, do you think being your father's son has affected your ideas or experiences relative to being a child of our Lord?

4. Picture yourself as a little boy, alone in a place where you spent a lot of time as a boy—maybe, as we've said, back in your old bedroom, sitting on your bed. Now imagine yourself as you are today, quietly approaching and then coming near that boy. Sit down beside him. Spend some time there, just being with him. How does that feel? What kind of vibe are you getting from him? Do you think it's true that you might owe an apology to the boy you once were for having ignored him for so long? If so, consider telling him about how, in order for you to meet the challenges of moving on and becoming an adult, you had to make decisions and do things that necessarily meant leaving him behind—that you did what you had to do in order to make sure that he was safe. Encourage him to talk to you. Tell him that you very much want him to tell you what it's meant to him, all these years, to have silently observed, and had no say in, your life. Really, really listen (and write down) every last thing that he says to you. Expect the exchange between you and him to last a good long time. Be sure to have a box of tissues nearby.

5. Share with your wife your understanding and discovery of your inner child. Tell her what it's meant to you to reclaim for yourself the boy you used to be. Share that boy with

her. See if she doesn't find that she, too, has an inner child, a little girl who'd like nothing more than to come out and play with the boy who is, after all, her very best friend in the world.

HUSBAND | 4

THERE'S ONE THING about you, dear reader, that we are pretty comfortable guessing: You are either married or single.

And we would further venture that you are really, really aware of whether you are married or single.

Now remember: We're professionals. Don't go around making guesses like that on your own. Someone could get hurt.

And what makes us so confident that you are acutely aware of your Life Position relative to a member of the opposite sex? Because you're a human. And as everyone knows, being over the age of, say, fourteen means being pretty obsessed with just about every aspect of your relationship to members of the opposite sex.

None of us can help being that way. It's how we are hardwired.

(Note: One of the things that might have developed in your life is that you never married—or did, but aren't married right now. Or you, or your wife, might be two months or six years into a second or even third marriage. There are lots of ways for individual lives to configure around the Big Dynamic of Coupledom, aren't there? Now, if you're single or divorced or recently remarried, might we humbly suggest that you read this "Husband" section anyway? Pretty much everything that's true about how men and women in relationships should treat each other remains true whether you're talking about a couple that's been together for twenty years or twenty minutes. Love is love. Respect is respect. Boundaries are boundaries. Stick with us, if you will.)

Flashback alert!

One time when John was in the fourth grade, he received a note surreptitiously passed while he sat in class utterly failing in his attempt to pretend like he cared about longitude and latitude, or what a molecule is, or something else surely helpful later in life. The note was from a girl in class whom we'll call Svetlana Goodlooken.

As far as John could judge such things, Svetlana was the most beautiful girl in the known universe. That's definitely what John and everyone else in his class thought, anyway. She looked like a little movie star. But shy. She was pretty much perfect.

"I want to meet you today after school behind the fence"— said the note—"by the orchard."

And that's when John learned you could have a heart attack at any age.

After school, with his legs shaking like a rubber band someone had plucked, John made his way to the fence, and there, as promised, standing in the dappled sun, with the gentle breeze moving her hair just so, was Svetlana.

"Hey," he said when he reached her.

"Hello," said Svetlana. There was a pause, and then she stepped up to him, placed a hand on his chest, leaned in, and pressed against his lips her own, which were unbelievably soft and warm. After Svetlana stopped kissing him, she stepped back. With her robin's-egg-blue eyes locked onto his, she tilted her head slightly and smiled. And that was when he had this precise thought: *Now I'm obsessed.*

Seriously. He says those are the exact words that appeared in his head, like a giant newspaper headline.

At that moment, he knew for certain that—instead of the all-star third baseman or highly decorated Air Force pilot that he'd always thought he'd be—he was born to be nothing less than Svetlana Goodlooken's boyfriend. His whole purpose in life was to love that girl until she died. (Or, as it turned out, until her family moved away about three months later.)

With Svetlana's kiss, John knew that he was born to be a boyfriend, basically.

As were you.

As were all guys.

And what that ends up meaning, of course, is that most of us were born to be husbands. Because, let's face it, you can only be a swingin' single guy for so long. *Especially* if you're Christian. The whole Christian universe is pretty much designed to get people of age married. And why not? Falling in love and getting married is biblical; it's natural; it's a good and healthy thing to find the woman who is perfect for you, marry her, and then see what the world and God have in store for you both.

Perfect! Domesticity *rules!*

Of course, it really does rule—and, like any absolute monarch who ultimately dominates anything and everything, marriage is . . . an absolute state. When you're married, you're married. Which means you're not single. Which means you're no longer free to, for instance, date other women. Which . . . you know. Those are the sorts of freedoms that you willingly exchange for the love of the woman you decide to make your wife—just as she trades her freedoms.

And then you and your beautiful bride live happily ever after.

Ahhhh. It's all so lovely, isn't it?

It is!

But what's also true is that after a while it comes to pass that you and your beautiful wife have been married for twenty or thirty years. And maybe along the way the two of you had children who are now teenagers who like to drive you crazy by wearing black lipstick and/or listening to music that sounds like violence put to a beat. Or maybe your children have left for college, leaving behind an infinite-seeming void. Maybe you and/or your wife have elderly parents you're now taking care of.

Maybe your career didn't quite pan out as you assumed it would back when you were nothing but bright ideas and a world of nerve.

Maybe your wife's going through menopause.

The point is: Things have really changed. Life, that weird and unwieldy beast, happened to you. And now here you are: first and foremost, a Middle-Aged Married Guy. So let's take a look at some of the more salient aspects of that fact.

HUSBAND GOOD RIDDANCE #1:
Being basically insane about sex

Sex is certainly one tricky subject, isn't it? Everything about it is astoundingly intense and mesmerizing.

Well. Look who we're telling. Like you don't know.

And that, actually, is the good news about sex and its vast array of attending issues: Finally, in middle age, you actually do know all about it. We can leave behind our lifetime of insecurities about what sex is, how it works, what it's supposed to mean to us, and on and on until it's hardly any wonder that so many young honeymooners spend their first night ever in bed together, crying.

But those sorts of days are long behind us, aren't they? Now we're older, and a whole lot more knowledgeable and secure than we used to be about sex and sexuality and how it relates to our relationship with our wife.

We sometimes hear about how it's a concern that men in middle age "suffer" a drop in their testosterone levels. Well, if that's a concern, then it's a concern when the waiter at your cabana on the beach brings you two mai tais instead of one. It's something just about every man can definitely adjust to. Having less testosterone in your system is nice. It's calming. It's pleasant not to be as vulnerable to storms that used to knock us around the block.

In middle age our relationships with our wives really can be so much more about love, and so much less about sex. The focus in bed can be on making love, not simply the end result.

HUSBAND GOOD RIDDANCE #2:
All the psychological baggage and lies that stop you from being the greatest husband in the world

This is probably the single best thing we leave behind as we move into the second half of our lives. In our younger years, we're very much concerned with how we come across. We're forever running an interior program that scans everything we do and say to see if it's supporting or degrading the image of ourselves that we're eager to foster and maintain. In that sense we're striving to fill shoes that we can't yet, shoes that we own and figuratively keep stashed in the back of our closet in the hopes of someday being able to wear and enjoy them.

This sort of thing is perfectly normal, in that almost all of it is driven by the fact that we are primarily social creatures.

But in our journey toward becoming the person we feel we should be, what naturally happens is that we sometimes purposefully engage in what, for lack of a better word, we may as well call lying. Maybe we lie when we're scared or feel trapped or figure it won't hurt anybody and will serve us some good.

Whatever the reason, it's wrong, and as Christians we're particularly attuned to that sort of transgression. But we're also human, and when we are young, we so often feel challenged and even overwhelmed by what's going on around us that every once in a while we tweak the truth or flat-out fib. Doing that is just part of learning to fit into the world, of the process by which we learn to forge for ourselves a steady, honest identity that ultimately works for us and for God.

We don't only on occasion lie to others, however; sometimes we lie to ourselves. We insist to ourselves that we already are the kind of person we want to become. We adopt a *persona* for ourselves—and then block from our conscious minds (and from our behavior, if we can) anything that undermines or contradicts that persona. It's part of the process of how young people grow into their adult identities.

And then life goes on. We grow older and eventually run into the woman God thinks we should marry. And with great joy and thanks to the Lord, we then embark upon a deep and personal relationship with the woman whose life he saw fit to combine with our own.

Despite ourselves, we jam up our precious relationship with everything in us that is false or angry or suspicious or in one way or another fundamentally . . . well, crazy. At the time, though, it doesn't *seem* crazy to us at all; it's just "who we are." But is it?

The truth is, when we're young, few if any of us *do* know much about ourselves. How can we, when we really haven't had that much time to learn about ourselves, find out who we really are, both in relationship to the world and our own personal past? All that stuff is extremely challenging to sort through and figure out. And the cruel truth about relationships is that the less you know yourself, the less you are prepared to be in a good one. (Of course, in this regard we Christians are especially fortunate: We have God to teach us who we are if we avail ourselves of his truth and open ourselves up in community. And hallelujah for that.)

One of the greatest things about middle age is that it's the time when you finally begin to realize that you really *do* know who you are. You *do* know what makes you tick. You *do* know what you like, what you don't, how you feel, how you don't, what you believe, what you don't. All of it. You have the knowledge it takes to create a marriage so blessedly happy and healthy that it really can be described as a holy matrimony.

And by middle age you grow into someone worthy of a relationship like that—not because you are a more perfect person but because you become a more honest person. Where you used to hide your fears and insecurities from your wife, you now share them with her. You explore them with her. Now you and she *together* define them, understand them, and make them go away.

And there you are: The best friend your wife ever dreamed of having.

(One final note on this, just because I can't talk about husband-and-wife best friends and that level of connection without pointing out one vital requirement: the commitment of all you are to her. You can't just commit to not touching someone else or to not ever having sex with anyone else. You must commit your eyes. You cannot look at pornography and develop a deep connection with your wife. The fact is that a real live woman just won't do it for you if you saturate your mind with the unreality of pornography. End of lust lecture.)

HUSBAND GOOD RIDDANCE #3:
Taking your wife for granted

We take our wives for granted. We know we do. We wish we didn't. But we do it anyway. We're too quick to show our wives anger; we too often treat them dismissively; we're not nearly as uncomfortable as we should be being curt and impatient and Generally Imperious with them.

Men. We can be such *wieners*, can't we?

While there's never a bad time to stop taking our wives for granted, middle age is particularly ideal to start treating them as the wonderful treasures they are. We are finally able to gain the perspective necessary to see them as people entirely separate from us—in a way we haven't really done since the days when we started going out with them.

Remember how, when you first met your wife, you *never* took her for granted? What happened to those days? What happened to that respectful, loving buffer that first existed between you and your would-be wife, that Never Militarized Zone wherein, via instinct and inclination, you made sure that just about every talk the two of you had together was, if not an out-and-out loving talk, at least a peace talk?

Well, what happened, of course, is that the two countries formally known as [insert your name here] and [insert her name here] didn't just sign a Peace Accord—they actually merged into one country.

The two of you became one.

And even though it would make people cry for all the wrong reasons, shoe-horned into the traditional marriage vows—somewhere between "through richer and poorer" and "in sickness and in health"—should be "through constantly and egregiously taking each other for granted." Because, like it or not, it *is* part of the package that you sign up for on the day you get married, and it usually starts about five minutes after you eat the cake. That is why I recommend that couples not eat the cake. It changes everything.

Taking for granted someone with whom we spend so much time is to some extent a naturally reflexive response that simply can't be avoided. It's also simply a function of testosterone: We men *are* prone to impatience and imperiousness, because while those kinds of qualities might not be the best for cuddling on the couch and planning an afternoon tea, they're great for wrestling wild boars or chasing enemies off into the woods.

And the thing about *those* types of hyper-"testosterony" endeavors is that they are, mainly, a young man's purview. An older man—a man with some wisdom and experience—is more inclined to, if possible, leave the wild boars and his enemies to their own fate.

Why? Because the perspective of a man with some years behind him is necessarily broader than a younger man's. The man with experience is less inclined than a younger man to impose his will upon people and situations outside of himself; time has taught him the pleasures of simply respecting and reflecting what *is,* rather than worrying so much about what "could" or "should" be. And an older man also knows what a younger man hasn't yet learned: time changes things. The older man knows that sometimes it's best to rein back one's will and let time work its transformative magic.

One of the things that time changes about a man in midlife is that it brings him the perspective he needs in order to see both himself and his life more objectively. What an extraordinary blessing! And one of the best things about that blessing is that we come to see our wives more objectively, too.

Midlife is the time when God deepens and enriches our life experience by showing us that, after all, we don't know our wives anywhere near as well as we think we do. It's a time when God is ready to reveal to us that, just like we're changing, our wives are also changing—which means that between the two of us, there are a lot of new presents on the table, waiting to be unwrapped.

When it comes to a relationship based on a twenty- or thirty-year marriage, middle age is *the* great time of renewal and discovery. It's amazing to find out and explore what our wives are going through and thinking about in the middle years of their own lives.

And here we thought *we* were going through some big changes.

It turns out that midlife is the time when the Lord, in one way or another, says to us, "Surprise! Your wife is at *least* as complex and driven as you are. The girl's an ocean you've barely begun to fathom! Time to get *polite* again, boy!"

And sure enough: We look anew at our wives and see again someone whom we'd like nothing more in this world than to please and to be worthy of.

HUSBAND PURE GOLD #1:
The invaluable time you've spent with your wife

Time. The presses won't stop at this observation, but we only have so much of it. As an ancient Hindu mystic once put it, "Before you know it, you're dead."

Boy. Those ancient Hindu mystics really knew how to boil stuff right down, didn't they? Still, they are absolutely right: Before we know it, we really are outta here.

As we all know but perhaps don't often enough reflect upon, time is our most precious, most *irretrievable* commodity. When it's gone, it's gone. And that brutal fact must mean that how we actually spend our time here on earth truly counts for something.

And it does. In the final analysis, every second of our lives counts, because every moment can contribute to our overall understanding of life. For a lot of us that truth feels pretty counterintuitive. Most of us tend to think that if we spend an entire day, say, lying on our couch watching TV, then by definition we've "wasted" that day. Men are especially prone to this kind of thinking, this conviction that time not spent doing something "constructive" is time wasted. But in actuality, there is virtually no such thing as wasted time. If we spent a day on the couch doing nothing, we did that for a very real reason.

Though we may not have even been aware of it, maybe we spent that day on the couch because we were depressed. Maybe we were angry. Maybe our Inner Toddler was basically demanding to be indulged. Maybe we were simply exhausted. *Something* was going on with us. Something is always going on with us, fueling everything we do, say, think, and feel.

As the sages say, in every detail lies the universe. But you have to stop and look at the details to see if they form a pattern that might be helpful to break.

Because God made all of us in his image, it makes sense that a key way to understand at least something of God's nature is to know as much as possible about our own.

In terms of our nature, it's *all* about our relationships. And for most us, the Big Three of Relationships are those we have with our parents, our siblings, and our spouse. For only one of those do we actually have a choice.

We chose our wives; our wives chose us. And thus did each of us begin whole new lives for ourselves. And throughout our marriage, how have we really been spending our time with our wife?

Learning about God, that's what. Maybe not purposefully. Maybe not systematically. Maybe not even consciously. But throughout our relationships with our wives, God has always been working behind the scenes, teaching us about love, sacrifice, humility, patience, acceptance. Our marriages are there to teach us just about everything there is to learn in this life that's of real and lasting value.

By grounding ourselves in a relationship that's grounded in love, we've been every single day experiencing God in a way that's as direct and rich—and *certainly* as constant—as any other way available for us to experience him.

For better or worse, the time we've spent with our wives really *has* been the time of our lives; it is how we've physically spent so much of our time. And whether or not at any given moment we were aware of it, all of that time was, in fact, divine.

HUSBAND PURE GOLD #2:
Understanding the true value of compromise

Our highest purpose and goal in life should be to love and know God, right? And what do we all possess that deeply hinders the realization of that goal and purpose? Our ego-driven, stubbornly resistant will. Yes, our innate drive to impress ourselves on the world—to matter, to be important, to be the center of attention, to continuously desire that everything work out in a way that benefits or pleases us. It's the core human characteristic that Nietzsche identified as "the will to power."

Being by nature sinful—selfish, arrogant, greedy, imperious—we oftentimes don't want to "let go and let God": We want to do it all ourselves. We want to be King of the World. We want our will to reign supreme. We don't, in other words, want to compromise.

And then, at some point, we meet and marry the woman we fall head-over-heels in love with.

I believe that God uses marriage to open the hearts and minds of his believers to the reality of his nature, which John the Divine says *is* love. Marriage is when we really begin learning what God most wants us to learn: that love is bigger, better, and more important than anything *we* could ever hope to be or make of ourselves.

And what one thing is the key to a happy marriage?

Compromise. The ability and willingness to make your own will and your own needs subservient to love. Which is, to say, to make your will subservient to God's. Which is pretty much the Whole Point, isn't it?

God knows our needs. What we need more than anything is an everyday, readily comprehended, *love-based* means of understanding that life is *all* about learning to give up our personal will for his divine love.

It is our job to understand this is true.

It's God's "job" to help us understand that truth.

And how, exactly, does he go about doing that?

Kiss your wife the next time you see her.

She's how.

HUSBAND PURE GOLD #3:
Being your wife's hero

By nature we men are a modest lot. And that's as God intended.

(If you happen to be a woman reading this, we men would deeply appreciate it if you would at this moment stop sniggering so violently.)

We're modest.

We're humble.

We can't imagine anyone thinking of us as a hero. Because, God knows, we're not.

We can't be.

We never have been.

Except, here's the thing: Your wife sure *does* think about you being a hero. She can't help it. To her, a big part of who you are *is* a hero. You have—and more times than it's natural for you to be aware of—been your bride's hero. You remember some of those times, don't you?

That time when you successfully steered the car over onto the shoulder, and then right there on the side of the road changed that flat tire, maybe.

Or maybe that time you climbed onto the roof of your house to find out what was going on up there.

Or that time you helped that one old woman—or that blind guy or that kid on the bike or that cat stuck up in a tree.

All of those sorts of things, all of those kinds of times. None of that stuff is ever lost to your wife. She remembers it all.

Remember when you were young? Remember who you were when she met you? Remember how strong you were then? Remember how brash? How confident? How bold? How daring?

Well, guess what? *You* may have forgotten or rarely think about those times, but you better believe that's the "you" your wife still sees when she looks at you. Women are weird like that. Women are blessed like that. Women bless us like that.

Certainly in the past—and very likely in the Actual Present—you *were* the hero of your wife. And because love really is timeless, to her you still *are* that hero.

You know you're the man. You know you're her hero. You definitely know that you've *been* her hero.

Have you ever had a real hero that you fell out of love with? A hero whom you weren't at any moment ready to again accept as a hero? Well, neither has she.

Welcome to your life, Superman.

HUSBAND PURE GOLD #4:
Feeling/knowing how deeply God has always been with the two of you

We tend to live our lives fairly engrossed with whatever is holding or demanding our attention at the moment. Our present lives are complex and busy, which is certainly fine. If men weren't so terribly busy and engaged all the time, God only knows the kinds of trouble we'd get ourselves into.

We can't help it. We're . . . well, men.

And we're not *just* men, are we? We're married men. And the life of a married man is one of exceptional practical and emotional complexity, is it not? A big reason that's so is because women, as it turns out, are human.

Women are human. Men are human. And all of us excel at being Completely Complex.

The next thing we know, we and our wives are no longer young; instead, we're a middle-aged couple who take pleasure in doing nothing more complex than sitting on the couch together holding hands and watching a movie.

It's all about spending quality time with someone who's been with you over the long haul, isn't it?

That's because relationships are like fine wine. They're better with time. It's often difficult, for instance, to really understand whatever you and your wife are going through when you're in the midst of it. The present lacks context. It takes time before you can look back over and discern in your life patterns, dynamics, and relationships that you can't even begin to perceive or understand without that distance.

Your life is the medium through which God the Master Artist reveals the full scope and breadth of his creative, infinitely compassionate genius. And he just spent the last chunk of your life painting your life and marriage with his hues, textures, shapes, and perspectives. Middle age finally provides enough distance to view and understand it as the masterful work it is.

When you take hold of your wife's hand, and with her look back on your life together, what do you see?

You see Jesus. And you see him revealing himself to you in precisely the way that would mean the most to you, showing himself to you in the language that you're most attuned to understanding: through the details, emotions, mechanics, and dynamics of your regular, everyday, shared life.

People are forever wishing they had proof of God's existence, that they could just *see* Jesus, and thus know he is real.

And there you are, with your life; and there you are, with your wife.

If there is one thing about God that can be made absolutely clear to you, it's that he's every bit as real as the hand you hold when you're sitting together with your beloved wife on that beloved old couch of yours.

HUSBAND: Movin' On

In many ways, life is a fundamentally lonely proposition. Like the sage said: We're born alone; we live alone; we die alone.

Boy. And sages wonder why they don't get invited to more parties.

The biggest single thing that any of us ever does to counterbalance the whole Goin' It Alone thing that defines so much of our lives is to get married. That's it. That's the Big Join. Getting married is our proclamation to the world and to ourselves that we are optimists; it's how we manifest our conviction that not only can we be happy, but that we have what it takes to make a whole other adult person happy.

With a simple "I do," we claim as our own the truth that even though we may be born alone, and perhaps even have to die alone, we do *not* have to live alone.

Whoo-hoo! Bring on the cummerbunds!

But you know what happens, though? A lot of us get married, and then to one degree or another continue, emotionally if not physically, to be alone. There are of course a zillion reasons why, but they can probably all be boiled down to a single cause: At the core of our souls most of us harbor a conviction that no one in this world except for maybe God himself can ever know exactly what it is like—and means—to be us.

From the beginning you've wanted your wife (and your kids, your boss, your co-workers, your neighbors . . .) to think of you as being a certain sort of man: strong, together, successful, and so on. You want to be that kind of man. Every man does.

The problem, of course, is that you sometimes do or say things that we all imagine a truly honorable, self-sufficient, disarmingly wise and witty man wouldn't be caught dead doing.

You keep things about yourself hidden, basically. Not because you're bad or a liar or deceitful or anything like that—but just because you're *normal,* and normal people tend to prefer keeping to themselves those things that might give others a reason to think less of them.

We all act like the fallen, sinful creatures that we are. And then we hide the fact that we've acted like that. The selfish, greedy, fundamentally unnatural things that we do—the things that we tend to feel guilty for doing—are the things that we then keep secret from others.

And that's fine—or it would be, if it wasn't for the fact that once you've got a secret about yourself, then you've just made it true that no one on this earth but you *can* know you. They can know *some* of you; they can know *part* of you—but they can't know it all. Because in keeping a secret about yourself, you establish a part of you that is Absolutely Off Limits.

Which, again, is fine. Healthy, even. We must, after all, have some border between what we share with the world and what we don't. We can assume that our natural proclivity to keep some things entirely unto ourselves is just part of God's plan to make confession a big part of our relationship with him.

Here's the thing, though: It is perfectly reasonable to keep secrets from everyone but God, *except* when it comes to your wife. There's exactly one person on this planet who should know everything about you that you know, and that's the woman whose life you promised to fully cleave unto your own.

The reason it's so important to share things with your wife you might normally want to keep from her is a surprising one: *That's* where the really good stuff is. It's what makes us most human. Because what we hide usually isn't so much anything we've done but rather things that we feel. We keep hidden our most irrational worries, our wildest ambitions, our fervid dreams. We keep hidden all the "kid" stuff, basically, all the wild, crazy stuff that doesn't fit into our everyday, "normal" lives. And we keep that stuff from our wives because we think she'd really prefer *not* to be aware. We fear it might upset her if she knew that, secretly, we wanted to do this or that, or to pursue this, or to take a chance with that.

In a way, it's sometimes as if we're afraid that we've been so proficient at being the person we're supposed to be, that at this point we're afraid of being (if not actually knowing or exploring) the person we really are.

The house of our lives has been constructed. And we and our wives live in that house. Well, we tend not to want to rattle the windows of that house. And we sure don't want to upset its foundation. So we claim for ourselves a dark corner in the basement of that house, where we put the stuff that we don't want anyone else to know about.

I (Steve here) have a friend named Dan, who owns and runs a car repair shop. If you go into Dan's office just off his garage and look in the space between the wall and his filing cabinet, you will find there an electric guitar and a portable electric guitar speaker.

Sometimes late at night, after the day's work is done and the garage is locked up, Dan goes into his office, pulls out that guitar and speaker, plugs everything in, kicks back in his chair, and plays. Back in high school and for years after, Dan played in a rock band. They used to play bars and stuff. Dan's a good guitarist. He plays some of Clapton's stuff like he wrote it.

Dan's wife, Sue, has no idea Dan even owns that guitar. Dan doesn't tell her because he's sure she wouldn't like the idea—that she'd think it was his way of holding on to the rock 'n' roll demon he used to be. And that wouldn't work for her, which means it wouldn't work for Dan, either.

This way, everything remains within the Comfort Zone. Dan plays alone at night. Sue doesn't know. Everything's fine.

Except it's not fine. Because Dan's playing time really means something to him. It *does* bring him back to his rock 'n' roll heyday. It doesn't mean he wants to go out *now* and become Party Hearty Boy—but his guitar does represent a part of who he used to be.

Dan's a good guy; he was a good guy back when he was playing in a band. He's matured, the way we all have, but his character's always been about the same.

Most critical to what we're discussing here is that in his garage while he's playing at night, Dan writes music—little songs and snippets of songs. It's during these most private times—when Dan is essentially hiding in his office—that he gets to be purely and unrestrainedly creative. It's time he protects like a lion. Even though he never starts playing until his whole shop is closed at night, when he does, he *still* closes his office blinds.

And then there he is. Creating. Alone. While, ostensibly, working.

Not really so ideal.

I (Steve still) have another friend who *loves* a good cigar—but only smokes them when he's away from his house and wife. "My wife'd kill me if she knew I smoked cigars," he says. "She hates the way they smell. She won't even let me keep one in the house."

So, with his wife's permission, my friend goes to poker nights with his friends, or they all go out fishing together, or whatever—and he never even tells his wife how, for him, so much of the fun of doing "guy stuff" with his friends is nothing more sinful or troubling than simply enjoying a good cigar. He figures that when it comes to his occasional cigars, what his wife doesn't know won't hurt him.

Well, not only is it hurting my friend, it is hurting his wife. Our wives aren't supposed to be our mothers; they're supposed to be our friends. We don't have to pretend to be something we're not—and we especially don't have to hide something for their sakes. If we know there's something about ourselves that would cause our wife pronounced discomfort—then we've got to tell her about that thing anyway, so that we can *talk* with her about it, so that we can share with her our conviction that whatever that thing is, it's not worth being dishonest about.

The reason it's so vital to do this is because middle age is all about not having to pretend anymore. Young people need to pretend about who they are because they haven't yet had time to become whoever they're going to be. Well, we *have* had time to become ourselves—and *now* it's time to share the entirety of who we are with the woman who has done so much to form and nurture that very person.

Midlife is all about Show 'n' Tell, man.

And do let us be clear: We're not saying you aren't already perfectly close to your wife. We know you have always known how important it is to share and communicate everything with the woman you love. All we're really saying is this: Take inventory. Make sure that you pull everything out of that little corner down there in your basement—and then sit down with your wife, and with her go through every single thing you found there. You're gonna pull out a baseball glove, or an astronomy chart for looking at the night skies, or a microscope that as a kid you used to love looking into. . . . There might be a guitar there or a cigar—or maybe even (gasp!) *sex* stuff!

Bring it all out! Talk about it! Share it! Pray about it! Get embarrassed about it! Be honest about it!

This is your *friend* you're going to be talking to. Not your mom; not your dad; not a cop; not your sister; not a schoolteacher. Your friend.

And what are friends really good for? Having fun, that's what.

If you believe nothing else about middle age, believe that at its core it's all about finally giving yourself permission to relax and just have some flat-out fun in your life.

Isn't it just possible that Dan's wife Sue always wanted to be a singer in a band? Is it so unlikely that maybe *she'd* like to play an instrument, too? Couldn't she at least be a groupie of Dan's? Couldn't there be something about Dan's guitar playing that would work for her? Isn't it possible that it would break Sue's heart to know that her husband felt that he had to keep from her something as precious to him as his musicianship?

Is it so outrageous to guess that, in fact, she'd be willing to take responsibility for whatever in the past she'd said or done that contributed to his thinking he needed to hide his playing from her? If she really thought about why, if it's true she's uncomfortable with Dan's guitar playing, might she come up with something that would be really healthy for her and her husband to acknowledge, validate, and explore together? Might not Dan's playing be something around which he and Sue could really bond?

Isn't it possible that my other friend's wife might actually like the way a good, sweet cigar tastes? That she might enjoy the little buzz it brings? Or that she might like playing a little poker with the guys, too?

We men really, really want two things out of life: To be loved for exactly who we are, and to have fun. The important thing to remember—the thing that can be a little tricky for us to remember—is that that's also exactly what our wives want.

HUSBAND: Things to Do

1. Tell your wife to think up five things about herself you might not know. And then, for five nights in a row, for at least an hour at a time, she gets to tell you all about each one of those things. Ask if she'd be willing to do the same with five things about you.

2. Talk to your wife about what you're going through these days; and talk to her about all of it, too—not just the parts that make you look good or seem especially set upon, or whatever. Unload, dude. Tell her things you might have imagined you'd never tell anyone at all. And if you find or feel that you can't be 100-percent open with her, talk to her about that. See whether or not the two of you can't figure out why you'd rather carry some burdens alone than share them with the one person in life with whom you're supposed to share all of your burdens and all of your cares.

3. Next time you find yourself expressing anger toward your wife, stop and think about how at that moment you're feeling about yourself. See if it isn't true that the reason you're snapping at her is because of something inside of you about which you feel acutely uncomfortable or (usually) guilty. It's an instant sort of impression you're after: It's not like you're going to have to sit down and think for half an hour about what you've recently done that's not only gnawing at you like a bear but making you act like one, too. Pretty

instantly, you'll know what you're unhappy with yourself about. And then tell her what that thing is, and apologize for mistaking being angry with yourself for being angry with her. Do that and then see if that moment doesn't turn out to be the best fight the two of you *never* had.

4. Consider whether or not you're satisfied with you and your wife's sex life. If you are, beautiful. But if not, make a list of the reasons why. Be honest; don't be shy or hesitant about what you write down. Do you wish the two of you made love more often? Do you wish that when you did, it was sometimes more spontaneous? Are you bored in bed; do you wish your encounters with your wife had more variety to them? Perhaps there's something specific you'd like you and your wife to try sometime. Write it all down.

   Once you have that list in hand, ask yourself whether you'd share it with your wife. If you would, then by all means, talk to her. (Be sure to acknowledge how basically embarrassing it is to talk about this stuff.) Sex, after all, isn't really about sex at all; it's about love. And love is largely about trust. Use the list to make yourself more vulnerable to your wife; share it with her as a means of proving how much you trust her. Who knows? You may end up with a variety of reasons for which you're glad you shared your list with her.

   If you wouldn't talk to your wife about what's on your list because you're afraid of her response, then consider the two of you going to see a marriage counselor. Marriage counseling isn't just for devastated marriages; any couple can benefit from it at just about any point in their relationship. Almost all problems in a marriage can be resolved through constructive communication—and sex is easily one of the most difficult things for couples to talk about. So seek some help. You don't want anything as important as your sexual lives to be something that you and your wife never *really* talk about. Instead of allowing it to be a block between you, use the difficulties you have talking with your wife about sex as a means of ultimately bringing the two of you closer together than ever.

PROVIDER 5

ONE TIME I was at a party talking to a guy from France, and he said to me, "You know, in Europe, when you begin a conversation with someone you've just met, you ask them how they are doing, how they are feeling, or what is going on just then in their lives. But here in America, you ask each other something entirely different."

"What's that?" I asked, somehow fearing the worst.

"Here," he said, "you ask, 'What do you do for a living?' In Europe, a person is defined by who they are. In America, a person is defined by what they *do*." His tone left no doubt as to which he thought was superior.

Ol' François (who was actually a really nice guy) had a point. We do define ourselves by what we do. And it's pretty difficult to imagine *not* doing so, isn't it, since we spend so much of our time working (not to mention thinking about it). Asking us not to define ourselves by referring to our Actual Job is like asking a monkey not to define itself by referring to the fact that it has long arms and fur and enjoys bananas.

Providing for those whose lives are cleaved to our own is something that we men take very seriously. For sure, if the scientists who spend all their time studying our genes just keep looking, sooner or later they'll find a little cluster on the male genome line that's stamped, "Bacon, Bring Home. Must Feed Family."

We *do* care about lugging home the pork; our identities and security are deeply tied to our jobs. And that's necessarily so: As much as it's ever been, it's a jungle out there, and money is how we and our families survive it. You better believe it's something we care about. Like we care about breathing.

I remember when I had a financial goal of making a thousand dollars a month. Well, there was a time when that could get you a pretty nice house, and a boat that at least would not sink. Now the financial goals are much different. There is no dollar amount attached. It doesn't really matter to me all that much. What I want more than money is to be able to keep doing what I am doing. Money gives me more choices, but it can never fulfill me like my ministry, like speaking, like writing this book, like raising my kids and being loved by an amazing wife. But like it or not, money is a reality that will not go away.

So the sooner we all learn to deal with some of the realities of it all, the better.

So, as we've been doing, let's step back for a moment and take a look at how our work lives have thus far been good for us, how they've been bad, and what we can do as we move into the second half of our lives to ensure that not only do we continue to support our loved ones but that we're also able to do so in a way that we find perfectly, and personally, rewarding.

PROVIDER GOOD RIDDANCE #1:
Defining yourself by whatever's written on your business card

Most of us get our first real career-type job in our early twenties—when we're just out of college or first trying to establish for ourselves an independent place in the world. By that time most of us are acutely aware of how vital it is that we *have* a job or career; we already grasp the difference between having and not having money. And most of us, of course, prefer having money. Which means getting a job—an intimidating challenge, since lack of experience automatically puts young people at a disadvantage in the marketplace.

So what do we do? We take the best job we can find. And then—especially if it happens to be a job we actually want—we hang on to that job like a wolf clamped on a lamb chop.

It's *money*. Plus, at that age it's hardly like we know exactly what we're doing out in the world, is it? We're just out there, paddling wildly, trying not to drown. We've barely had time to establish any sort of real identity for ourselves.

And then—pretty much on our first day of real employment—we suddenly *do* have an identity! We're guys with whatever job we have!

Voilà: We are men at last. With an income. And a place we're supposed to go to every day and a bunch of stuff we're supposed to *do* every day once we get there. Just like that, we have ourselves a life.

And because our work life is so big and important to us, we *really* identify with the job upon which we almost can't help but feel our very lives depend.

And just about all of that vital, wide-ranging dynamic is encapsulated in our business cards.

I'm "Tom Wickley, Assistant Process Manager." I'm "Robert Atkinson, Sales and Service."

"Ken Pullem, Customer Relations."

"Kyle Landley, Assistant Manager."

It's all there; it really *is* in the cards. And to a considerable degree, our jobs become who we are. And not just as far as doing our taxes or having to regularly dry clean our work clothes goes, either. We identify with our jobs at a level much deeper than those sorts of things. And why is that?

Hmm. Let's think.

Well, what's the most important thing that you have to do in a new job—or in any job at all, for that matter? Please the boss.

The boss is the absolute authority at work. The boss makes the rules; the boss enforces the rules. The boss is also usually operating with a very clear agenda in mind. It very often feels as if the boss can and will ruin your life if you don't get on board with that agenda, if you don't claim it as your own and do everything within your power to foster it along.

On the other hand, if you make of yourself the person whom your boss most wants you to be—you will be rewarded. Your boss will say things to you like "Atta boy!" and "Good work!" You'll get patted on the back, maybe singled out for praise. You'll be held up as an example to your co-workers (*siblings*). You're very likely to even get a raise in your salary (*allowance*).

You'll be someone whom you *know* your boss (*parents*) will be glad they hired!

Perhaps you see where we're going with this.

Whenever any of us gets involved in an intense and prolonged group dynamic in which we have a great deal at stake, it can't help but push in us a lot of the same emotional buttons that were installed in us the first time we were *ever* involved in an intense and prolonged group dynamic in which we had a great deal at stake. Our early family life goes a long way toward determining how we feel and respond to our work "family." And it sure had that influence when we were nearer in time to our original emotional paradigms—back when we were first making our way out into the job market.

Our boss wants to know how we're doing on that marketing report.

Our parents wanted to know how we were doing on our book reports.

Our boss evaluates and judges our best efforts to please him or her.

Our parents evaluated and judged our best efforts to please them.

Our boss tells us what time we have to be back from lunch.

Our parents told us what time we had to be in for dinner.

We're very often in effect competing with our siblings for the affection of our parents.

Who *doesn't* want the boss to like them best?

So, yes: The bottom line is that we definitely identify and are deeply tied up with our jobs and careers. As such, it's easy to become overzealous about our work life. We do that because what we tend to want out of a job—especially the first in our career—goes a lot deeper than having enough money to pay our bills.

In large part, we want to be validated by that job. We want to be comforted by that job. We want to be worthy of that job. And (probably more important) we also want that job to be worthy of us.

Our jobs just mean so very much to us.

And that makes sense. But in the final analysis, what we do for money—no matter how much of our physical and emotional time and energy it consumes—remains a pretty narrow trough running through one big field. It can be a *deep* trough, though. From where we sit, it's just walls on either side of us, the ground below, the strip of sky above, and that's it. That's what we live in. That's what we do every day. That's our work-a-day universe.

The great thing is that the older we get, the increasingly shallow our work trough becomes. Usually without our even noticing it, the floor along which we're running begins to angle ever so upward. And we keep working and running, and working and running, and all the while without knowing it moving closer and closer to ground level. And then one day, our head rises above the walls of our trough—and what do we see all around us but a beautiful, wide-open meadow.

Wow, we think. *This is great up here.* And we look back at the long and narrow ditch in which we've been so long endeavoring, and think, *What I've been doing there was good, productive work. It had to be done; it got me somewhere. But before I go back into that trough-that's-almost-a-tunnel, maybe I'll step out of my trough and walk around for a while! Maybe I'll dig myself another trough out there somewhere. Maybe I'm done running around in troughs! Who knows? All I know is that it sure is beautiful out here! A little scary maybe, but this is really nice.*

Ah, middle age. It's so great, the way it's just designed to lift us up, to unfold before us the view of a new meadow, the view of a new sky.

PROVIDER GOOD RIDDANCE #2:
The crazy-making gossip and personal politics of the workplace

If there's one thing you can say about jobs, it's that they often involve lots of interacting with other people.

And if there's one thing you can say about other people, it's that they sure do act pretty crazy when they're in their place of employment.

We've seen why: We understand that a person's job is inextricably bound to virtually everything that's critical to their understanding and experiencing of themselves. Our work is enmeshed with our sense of emotional security, our physical security, our vast array of self-esteem "issues." So of course we're all at least a *little* nuts when it comes to our job.

Put a bunch of people together, people who are *extremely* interested in what's going on around them and how every little thing will affect them, and what does it *do*?

It makes them talk. It makes them scheme. It inspires us all to . . . gossip and politic.

It's exhausting. It's harrowing. *That's* the stuff that keeps us awake at night. *That's* the stress about work. It's never the actual work that poses such a big problem for us; it's our co-workers who drive us so crazy.

The great thing about being middle-aged, though, is that by now you have so much experience working with so many different people that you're in a position to emotionally and intellectually separate yourself from the nonsense. Of course, none of us can ever completely ignore or be immune to the realities of office politics—but after twenty or thirty years, we've reached a point where we understand the nature of office politics and gossip. What finally sinks into us is that all of the "Guess what?" and "Did you hear . . . ?" stuff never really amounts to a hill of beans.

It's just people's way of keeping themselves excited and agitated and . . . dramatized.

PROVIDER PURE GOLD #1:
Knowing that when push comes to shove, you know how to work

A lot of times it's difficult for us to feel like we have as much control over our lives as we'd like. So much of what determines our experience is beyond our influence. We can't control what mood our boss or co-workers are in; the stock market shoots around like spinning tops in a wok; our cars suddenly decide they want to help with the environment by making us walk or take the bus to work, etc.

Of course it is a real comfort to know that God is watching over our lives and that ultimately everything will be all right. But let's face it: When the company putting together the graphics package for the huge presentation you're making that afternoon calls at the last minute to say they've accidentally ruined your materials, you're probably, at that moment, not going to be thinking all that much about God. (Wondering if he could take a moment to *smite* a person or two doesn't count.) Instead, you're going to be fixated on the reality before you. You're going to roll up your sleeves and get to work.

God's got his will, for sure. To that we add good ol'-fashioned work—using the muscles in our back and the sweat of our brow—to achieve most everything we want down here in this world he made for us.

Well, the great thing about being middle-aged is that we *have* worked. Most of us have worked more hours than we'll ever know. It's in our blood now; the work we've done is as much a part of who we are as are our shoulder blades and our legs.

We *know* from a hard day's night.

And that's an eminently comfortable thing to know, too, because life doesn't slow down—even in midlife. Instead, our lives get more complex and dynamic every day. And just as it could be back when we were young, that can still be fairly intimidating for us today.

The good news, though, is that it can't be *as* intimidating. Back then we had no idea what we were capable of. Now we do.

And because we do—because we can look back over our lives and see how many times, and under how many different kinds of adverse conditions, we've accomplished something important—we're not nearly as afraid of the world as we used to be.

Yeah, the world can be a big, bad place. But next to us? And our will? And the way we know how to work? And with *God* on our side?

Please. At this point, we should all leave our houses every morning with one hand tied behind our back, just to keep things fair between the world and us.

PROVIDER PURE GOLD #2:
The value and joy of true teamwork

Being on a team—a real team, one with a clear goal toward which everyone on that team is working their hardest—is one of life's greatest pleasures, isn't it? There's just nothing like it. It's one of the reasons we men are so fond of football. As a team out on the field you strategize; you execute a play; you gain some yards or you don't—but either way, you huddle up and do what, in one way or another, all great teams *must* do to succeed: In unison you all bend over and stick your rear ends out at the rest of the world.

Thus refocused on who you are and what you're doing, you all then "Break!" and have back at it.

Understanding team dynamics—what a team is, what it should be, what it can't be if it's going to have any chance of success—is valuable knowledge. In virtually any endeavor involving others—from our job to our home to our church to our community—a true knowledge of teamwork can be used to enhance the situation. Our whole country, for that matter, is supposed to be a team; ultimately, every person in the world is on Team Humanity.

Well, until the day when everyone on the globe actually realizes that truth, it should comfort us to know how much our personal experience has taught us the value of the team paradigm. Even if we don't think we can use that knowledge in a "practical" way—if "all" we do is sometimes reflect upon what it's meant to us to have belonged to great teams—we have something of incalculable value. And most of us learned a *lot* of what we now know and understand about teams through the different kinds of professional situations in which we've found ourselves over the years.

Good companies are *all* about teamwork. That's the bottom line. That's what'll *determine* the bottom line. As everyone knows (and as too many of us have probably experienced), a company begins to fail when employees feel they're not on a team they can believe in. Then they just don't care anymore. Then things start falling apart.

But, oh, a genuine team! Where people really care! When everyone knows they're part of a group that's working for something *beyond* the sum of them together! Where people can really and truly say they have pride in what they do every day!

A lot of us in midlife are in a phase where our careers—for myriad reasons—are, or feel, more unsettled than we'd prefer. If that's happening to you, this is a really good time for you to focus on those talents and powers of yours that *belong* to you—that will forever remain with you, no matter what gets merged, downsized, outsourced, or restructured. And one truly valuable life skill you've acquired "simply" by working as long as you have is the nature and value (and, sadly, the rarity) of a true team environment.

Right now, my New Life team is so much of a team that we have become more of a family. If someone has an idea, someone else instantly is trying to figure out how to make it happen. We care for each other and we care for those we minister to. All of which has left me not wanting to ever work with anyone who can't be a team player. Me, when I was younger, for instance.

Teamwork is a great thing to know and understand. It's great to know for work. It's great to know for family. It's one of the best things to know as a Christian.

The Lord Jesus Christ! Talk about the best boss any of us ever had.

Talk about being on the winning team.

PROVIDER PURE GOLD #3:
Knowing that people ate because of you

One nice thing about having a job is that sooner or later someone has to fork over some Actual Cash in exchange for your time and energy. *Whoo-hoo!* The great thing about cash is that you can trade it for stuff you *need* in order to get you up the next morning and off to work, so that you can put in the effort that'll bring you the cash to buy what you need to get back to work the next day.

And then the weekend comes!

And then you're off to work again!

And then you die.

Whoo-hoo!

Actually, that's not bad, is it? The money you've made over your lifetime didn't keep just you alive; it fed, clothed, and housed your family. That fact is so basic we almost forget it—or at least not very often feel the full weight and significance of it.

Well, feel it now! Let the glory of what you've done wrap around you like God coming down to thank and embrace you. Because of you, people you love ate. Because of your efforts and dedication, Actual Sustenance was produced and consumed; life continued because of you.

That's God's work! And you did it! Think of the solid, life-affirming good you've done in this world through your hard work.

The thing about men is that we tend to judge ourselves harshly. We're usually a lot more clear about things we *haven't* done than about things we have. A lot of us are nagged by feelings that when it came to our loved ones, we could have done more: We could have worked harder; we could have made more money; we could have been more emotionally or even physically available. Some of that may be true. But what's also *got* to be true is that if you've ever worked a day in your life, you've been of absolute service to everyone you know, and to a ton of people you never will. All work feeds back into the system and becomes part of the means by which other people make their living. There's no such thing as bad or wasted work; it's all grist for the Common Mill. (Unless you're, like, a pornographer or drug dealer—in which case your work *is* bad.)

As a race, we're still primarily about survival. Your work has helped with that survival. It's either largely or wholly kept you and your loved ones alive and well. It has contributed to the well-being of countless people unknown to you. You *did* bring home the bacon, Jack. And we know you're not done doing it yet.

PROVIDER: Movin' On

Okay—so what have we middle-agers really learned from all the years we've spent working? Moreover, what can we learn about our ongoing Imperative to Provide that will help us move into the second half of our lives in a way that's maximally beneficial for ourselves, our family, and our God?

Well, our vote for Best Life Lesson About Work is . . . (drum roll, please!): faithfulness.

God always has provided for us, hasn't he? We're still *here*, aren't we? Things may have been tough at times, but looking around twenty and thirty years later, we and our families have pulled through, right? And we all know to whom we're in debt for that, right?

By now we should have faith that God will *always* provide the means by which we can provide for ourselves and our families. We should trust that if we listen to him and follow in the direction he is forever pointing us, his provisions will not only be pleasing to him but will also satisfy us in ways we can barely imagine.

Steve (John here, writing about Steve) is actually a perfect example of a man who is deeply and truly satisfied with his work. He and his gang at New Life Ministries support the ministry of Jesus on earth, it's work ideally suited to Steve's nature, and it puts food on his family's table.

Some people are fortunate enough to know early on what exactly they want to spend their lives doing. If you are such a man, you already know what an ever-giving blessing that is. And yet, all of the blessings your career has thus far brought you will *pale* beside what's coming next: Our Official Permission to skip the rest of this section.

And you thought getting *paid* meant something. This is actually getting out of *reading*. Don't get too used to it, though—start reading again at the end of this section, at this chapter's "Things to Do." You'll still find something good for yourself there. But other than that—go on!

Okay: If you're a guy in midlife currently having a problem with your career or profession, that problem is likely to fall into one of these categories: (a) You want to switch careers and you know what you want to do next; (b) You want to change careers but don't know exactly what you'd like to do next; or (c) You like your job but fear you're getting squeezed out of it.

All right. Let's see how each of the aforementioned situations might be positively impacted through remaining faithful to the conviction that God *always* provides what those who love him need most.

You want to switch careers and you know what you want to do next. If you haven't yet, talk to your wife about the career change, no matter how outlandish-seeming or different it is. See what she says. Pray hard and long about the change. If your wife supports it, and you feel God's pleasure in it, then move heaven and earth to make it happen. (If you feel God's calling you to something that your wife *doesn't* believe is the best thing for you both, then you've come to an interesting moment. Someone's missing something somewhere. Don't move on your career change until you and your wife together figure out what that something is. It's *sharing* time with your bride, for sure.)

If a career change means becoming poorer for a while, then do that. But be careful about going We Can Only Eat Top Ramen for a Month poor. If your family will likely experience Actual Hardship, be *extremely* sure God is telling you to make the switch. (Don't put yourself in the position to explain something along the lines of, "You know, I thought I was supposed to make a living selling sock monkeys at outdoor fairs. Sorry! Maybe instead of 'sock monkey,' God was saying something about 'stock market.'") Above all, be faithful. Trust in God, even when it feels like you're running straight for a cliff. If you're sure he's put it in your heart to do exactly that, then aim for that cliff with all your might. Trust that God will catch you. If you're doing what God wants, do it with all the faith in him you know he deserves. Don't let him down.

You want to change careers but don't know exactly what you'd like to do next. This one's easy. Pray. (Is there any question to life where that *isn't* the answer?) Middle age is one of the best positions in life, because you're so open to life's possibilities. Trust that the Fuzzy Vision with which you may be viewing your career will soon clear up. God is aware of what is best for you to do with the rest of your working life. So are you, you just don't *know* you know it yet. And that, of course, is where praying comes in.

"Praying" isn't really the right word for this kind of interaction with God, is it? *Listening* is more like it. You just want to sit down, close your eyes, take a few deep breaths, and start hanging out while God, Jesus, and the Holy Spirit do that wondrous Three-in-One thing within you. Avail yourself of this transformative phenomenon for, say . . . what? Five minutes at a time? Ten? Twenty? Either way, it won't be long before you're on your way toward figuring out what you're supposed to do next. Be prepared, of course, for a blinding vision that sends you into the wilderness—or at least a gentle nudge or two that sends you on a few exploratory trips: a night class, a volunteer opportunity, talking with someone in the profession you're interested in. It may take a while—and when it does happen, it might not happen with Old Testament–style drama and certainty—but trust that eventually, through prayer, you'll hear your calling calling you.

You like your job but fear you're getting squeezed out of it. *This* is tough. This is where you have to gather together everything you know about what you do for a living, break it down into its component parts, and then (as creatively as you need to) reassemble those parts into something you can use to make sure you come out of your current situation stronger than ever.

The main thing is not to let yourself get trapped in a rut. If things around you are changing, you've got to position yourself so that those changes work for you. You don't want to be just waiting for a bus to hit you; you want to prepare yourself to jump on that bus when it goes barreling by.

Remember that you *know* stuff. By now you've acquired real, experience-based wisdom in and about your field. This might be the time for you to start making that fact clear to others. One way to do that is by conceiving and proposing initiatives and ideas forged from your wealth of knowledge and understanding about what *is*, in fact, best for your company. (And what's also, should it come to it, best for your company's competitors.) A lot of us these days are suffering from the stigma born of the culturally cultivated, media promulgated conviction that old faces equal old ideas. Maybe you're the guy who starts helping people in your company understand that from old faces can *also* come truly inspired, wise ideas.

Nine out of ten times, winning in a fluid situation boils down to boldness. And effective, career-enhancing bold moves boil down to creative thought, thorough preparation, and confidence. Get all three of those pistons firing, and the sky's the limit. So let's look at each real quickly:

1. **Creative thought:** You *think* of the ideas and proposals mentioned above. No big deal. You probably know twenty or thirty things right now that are wrong with your company and need fixing. Pick two of them. Claim them as your own. Fix them. Use them as your starting blocks.

2. **Thorough preparation:** You actually *produce* well-written proposals that can't help but bring you power. You master technologies that are important and new to either you or your field. You discover, prove, and assert the potential of resources that others have either long ignored or never even knew existed. Where others speculate with guesses and conjecture, you analyze with facts and data. You do the work necessary to establish yourself as someone any company would be crazy not to capitalize on.

3. **Confidence:** Remember, you're always a part of the team that consists of you, your wife, and God. You're not in this alone. United, you stand.

Mostly, just have faith. If you *are* getting squeezed out of your job, and there's nothing you can do about it, trust that God's using the situation to bring you somewhere that he's decided you need to be. Update your resume. Alert yourself to the possibilities around you. Remain optimistic. Remain faithful.

PROVIDER: Things to Do

1. With a pad of paper before you, imagine yourself quitting or walking away from whatever it is you currently do for a living. Then, while the emotional reverberation of that decision is still within you, write down all the thoughts or feelings that come to you. You might write, for instance, "Fear. Panic. We'll starve. Ashamed," and so on. Just quickly write down whatever jumps into your head, without thinking about it at all. It's not like there are wrong things to write down here. Just free-associate, man.

   When you're done writing down all the thoughts and feelings that leaving your work evinced in you, divide what you've written into two categories: Feelings and Real. Put under Feelings those things you wrote down that are, well, feelings: "Fear. Panic. Relief. Desperation," or whatever you have. Then move under Real those things that reference real, tangible life: "Can't pay mortgage. Can't feed family. Sell pool table?" and so on.

   For now, put aside the stuff that you've got categorized as Feelings, and look at what you've listed under Real. Taking one item at a time, very seriously ask yourself how *real* each really is. It's likely that most of what you've classified as "real" has to do with the Actual, Physical Ramifications of your suddenly losing your job or income. What you want to do now is ascertain the degree to which those concerns are in accord with the mechanics of what actually happens in everyday life. And for each of your listed concerns, do not fail to rationally evaluate their worst-case scenarios, either—because in the end, that's where real panic comes from, isn't it? It's the possibility of the *worst* thing happening that really freaks us out, right? So you'll want to be sure to look all the way down each of those dark tunnels. If, for instance, you scribbled down, "We'll starve!" then think about how realistic that is. If you lost your job tomorrow, would your family *really* starve—or would you instead be able to put together a plan in which it's unlikely you or any of your loved ones would actually perish from lack of sustenance?

If you wrote down, "Can't pay rent!" or "Can't make mortgage!" then ask yourself how true that really is. If you really couldn't pay the rent or mortgage, for instance, then follow through what would actually result from that. Would you really get kicked out of your residence? When, exactly? By whom? If it actually came to pass, wouldn't that whole process take long enough for you to come up with a contingency plan and avoid being homeless?

Go through your whole list like that, basically isolating what amounts to your ungrounded fears from the real situations that triggered those fears. Then ask yourself this question: Where did those fears *come* from? What are they based on, anyway?

Why did you feel (if you did) that you and your dependents would starve?

Why did you feel (if you did) that you and your family would actually be wandering around the streets at night, looking for a place to sleep?

And what about the emotional responses you have listed under Feelings? Do you find some of that stuff to also be sort of . . . overblown? That some or all of it's more intense than would actually be warranted by the fact of your losing your job?

Again—why *is* that?

What are all these fears really about, do you think?

Do you think maybe God allows us to fear specifically because he appreciates how fears can very suddenly and deeply make us aware of our absolute, utter dependence upon him? And in the end, isn't it true that if you and your family have God, you really *do* have all you need? Because he *always* provides enough to those who faithfully believe that he will?

2. Make a list of every boss you ever had and pretty seriously disliked. Underneath the name of each, write down what made that person such a nightmare to work for. And then

consider what you did to adapt and survive relative to each one of those jobs and bosses. See what effect making and reflecting on that list has on the way you feel about yourself and those jobs.

Now pat yourself on the back. Because are you one serious *survivor,* or what?

3. Make a list of what, when you were a kid, you most wanted to be when you grew up. Think about why those jobs and aspirations were so attractive. Now think about your current job or career. In what ways have you incorporated into your current work the qualities that meant so much to you as a kid? Do you find at all surprising the degree to which you are, in fact, living the dream?

4. Spend some very real time answering this question: If you never had to work another day in your life—if, say, you suddenly won the lottery—how would you spend your time? What exactly would you do with your life if you were financially free to do what you pleased? Think about what your answer to that question says about how you feel and think about your life these days. Is the life you're leading *way* out of accord with what you'd do if you could do anything at all? Is it not that different? Is it possible that you're already doing the very thing you would choose to do if you had absolute freedom?

Maybe you're happier with your chosen career than you know. Maybe you're less happy with it than you allow yourself to know. See if your answer to the theoretical question we've posed doesn't reveal to you something concrete that you could use to enhance your *un*-theoretical workaday life. One final note here. It is easier to believe the green stuff is greener in a different job. But if you go get that position, you will be taking yourself with you and you may discover that it wasn't the job that needed adjusting. You already may be in the "perfect" job but just unwilling to look at your imperfections and go to work on them.

Okay, this really is the final note. Often we think we have to change jobs to do something significant. It is not true. We don't need more ministers on the mission field, we need more men making money and making a difference with it and making a difference in the lives of the people around them. Recently a man quit his multimillion-dollar position to be a missionary. After about a year he admitted he was a very lousy missionary. So he came back and got another multimillion-dollar job so he could send money to the guys who really were called to be missionaries. Get it?

FATHER

NOW THIS is a role I love. My first time stepping into this role was when I became the father of Madeline. I then took on a little different form of dadship when I became the bonus dad of Carter and James. And then when little Solomon came into the world at the same time other dads my age were celebrating grandfatherhood, it became such a wonderful new and improved experience. I am different now than the first time around, and the first time around I gave it everything I had. *This* time I am not just giving everything I have to the baby; this time I am also (drum roll here) attempting to give everything I have to the baby's mother. This is quite a difference that literally makes all the difference in the world.

Our entire life certainly becomes different when we take on the dad role. We instantly go from being a carefree, innocent guy enjoying the show from the sidelines to a guy who's suddenly supposed to start *starring* in the show as "Dad."

And right about then is when most of us, blinded by the lights, start frantically looking about for our own dad. *What happened to that trusted stage veteran?* we find ourselves thinking. *Where's the guy who really knows this part?!*

But it's too late for that; our own show must, after all, go on.

Of course, for most of us middle-agers, the First Father jitters are long gone. For a lot of us, in fact, our concern has changed from "I can't believe this little life is really dependent upon me!" to "I can't believe this fully-functional amateur adult really *isn't* dependent upon me!"

That's some change.

Kids. How *dare* they do the one thing we spent years beseeching them to?

How *dare* they grow up?

But, alas, they do.

And since I still have kids at home and will for another couple of decades, I am going to turn this section over to the all-wise and all-knowing John Shore.

If there is one thing being a parent teaches you, it's that Time Really Happens. When kids are little it's almost as if you could sit them down on the couch, take off their shoes and socks, and just watch their feet grow. That's the way of life; as everyone knows, God is clearly intensely interested in having life develop. And how.

Like a giant *whoosh* you feel going by you, your babies become children, become kids, become teens, become people with lives of their own—who *definitely* want to get together with you, just as soon as their midterms are over or all the craziness at their job subsides or they finish up with all the work they're doing on their new home.

And then there we are, with this . . . *gap* in our lives where our children used to be. And we don't know whether to laugh about how independent and *away* from us our grown children are now or to cry about the exact same thing.

So we do both, of course.

Change. You can't live with it; you can't have yourself dipped in resin and placed beside a picnic table in your kids' backyard.

All any of us can do is exactly what our kids have always done: Keep growing.

FATHER GOOD RIDDANCE #1:
The sheer, unending labor of raising young kids

Well, this was an easy first "Good Riddance" to choose. Even if your kids aren't fully grown and out of the house, isn't it still just about the greatest thing in the world that they can, for instance, put on their own pants without any help at all?

Raising children is work. And it's hardly the sort of work that sticks to any kind of schedule, is it? Instead, it's the kind of work that cries around the clock, that won't eat spaghetti unless it's cut into uniform lengths, that suddenly *has* to have your help on a school project that should have been started weeks ago, that causes you to pull out all your hair.

The scientists are right: Male pattern baldness *is* caused by genetics. It's caused by your kids.

Of course, most of the work involved with raising children isn't frustrating or emotionally difficult. Most of it's just . . . work. Raw, middle-of-the-night, No Rest for the Weary–type effort.

You're down; your child's up—and then you're up, too. No choice. No letup.

No control, really.

And that is why at one time or another every man with a wife who stays home to look after the house and children has pulled out of the driveway in the morning and praised God for his part of the Domestic Deal.

Most of us don't need Oprah or Dr. Phil to tell us how hard our stay-at-home wives work. They do more sheer work in three hours than we usually do in a day. We get that. Despite the amazing number of television commercials predicated upon the idea that we are, we're not entirely stupid.

The point is: For most of us dads (and moms), the really hard, sort of *physical* work of having children is over, or nearly so. Now our kids are grown; now they can do their own work, put themselves to bed, find their own jackets, cut their own spaghetti.

Still, don't you sometimes find yourself sitting at the dining room table, gently turning a knife or fork in your hand, wishing that you could hear one of your children, just one more time, ask you to reach over and cut their spaghetti just right?

FATHER GOOD RIDDANCE #2:
The burden of always having to be Super, Never-Wrong Dad

A lot of us have the depth of character and maturity not to fall into this trap—but for others of us, being a father triggers a compulsion to be Super, All-Knowing Father. You know? We can't just be regular guys; we have to be Dads Who Are Never Wrong.

Remember that guy at the zoo we talked about back in the He-Man chapter, the one who pretended like he was the world's expert on Malayan sun bears? *That's* the guy we too often feel like we need to be.

The truth is that for many of us, having children who look up to us to fulfill virtually all of their physical, emotional, and intellectual needs can be pretty daunting. But we can't *say* it's daunting; we can't *act* like it's daunting; we can't *admit* that half the time we barely have any more of an idea about what's going on than our kids do. We are men, which means we are the head of our families, and how would our *not* knowing stuff help anyone? Nobody wants a captain who isn't quite sure how to steer his ship. No one wants a medic who shows up at the scene of an accident, jumps out of his ambulance, and yells, "Does anyone here know first aid? Anyone?"

Of course, Being Comfortable Being Uncomfortable is yet another area in our lives in which being Christian makes the difference between emotional stress and genuine peace. Part of teaching our children about God is sharing with them the truth that we, just like they, are so far *beneath* God that there's no reason anyone should feel Large and In Charge. We're not, and our children are not; no mortal is. The best any human can ever be is Small and Ready to Obey.

Of course, it's only natural that we adults know so much more about life than our children do (a fact they would do well to understand and respect). But ultimately, it is not only okay but good to admit whenever something's got us emotionally, intellectually, or spiritually stumped. Some of us were or are better than others at sharing this precious admission with our children. The important thing to remember is that no matter how old our kids are, it's never too late to make ourselves vulnerable to them, to share with them how challenging we, too, sometimes find the world.

When they're small, our children can hardly help but think of us as superhuman. We see that they do, and then naturally try to be for them that very thing. We want to be the heroes that we know our children believe we are. The older our kids get, though, the more we can let that go.

In the trajectory of your relationship with your children, the glory is not in transforming from your true self into a superhero.

The glory, finally, is in transforming from a superhero into your true self.

FATHER GOOD RIDDANCE #3:
The burden of all those times you were something less than the Perfect Dad

Part of being a father is knowing that at times we have let our children down.

God knows we have, on occasion, done that.

And we know our children know it. Which is somehow even worse. Which, actually, is how it should be. It *should* be worse to be the hurter than to be the hurt.

We don't like to think about how, when, where, and over what we once disappointed or even flat-out hurt our children. We don't like to dwell upon it. Not helping is that we also, at the time of our offense, are not inclined to apologize for it.

Some of us are better at saying we're sorry than others, of course. But for most of us, apologizing to, say, a nine-year-old for speaking to him too harshly isn't exactly what we'd call our second nature. (Though, again, we Christian Dads really have an edge in the Being Humble department, don't we? If any guy can muster up the emotional wherewithal to apologize to a child, it's we CDs. On the other hand, let's face it: We're also prone to taking the whole "We're the head of the household" doctrine too far, leaving us particularly sensitive to the idea that we have erred.)

Even though we may not care to apologize to our children, we sure do tend to remember our wrongs. That's the burden of the conscience.

In truth, most of us have reconciled ourselves to the fact that we're only human; that things happen; that in the balance we're not just good parents but really good—maybe great!—parents. And our kids love us; they're all right. In one way or another they've made it clear to us that they really and deeply forgive us. They know that at times they've let us down, too.

We all know that all we've ever been is all that we can be: human.

Fair enough.

But here's the thing: If you're a middle-aged guy harboring any guilt involving your child, don't deny yourself or your child the tremendously relieving and even exhilarating gift of apologizing to them. There's no shame in doing that; there's never any shame in being truthful.

At the very least, bear in mind that you're certainly not the only parent who feels guilty for times they've been less than an ideal parent. At one time or another, we've all seriously blown it with our kids. It can't be helped—not that knowing that ever really helps.

What *does* help, as we Christians know, is to be forgiven. What helps is to be purposefully vulnerable to those we've hurt or wronged—to put ourselves in a position where we can, in fact, be humiliated, hurt, and rejected by them, if that's what they feel they need to do.

What helps is to do our best to make everything right again.

If you've got anything weighing on you about your relationship with a child of yours, talk with that child about it. Get it out in the open. Do and say everything you can to show that you accept full responsibility for the role you played in whatever hurt they feel was done to them.

No matter what you did in the past, you're still that child's father. And you *are* older. And that does make you wiser. And ultimately all wisdom points toward humility.

So be humble. Ask God to forgive you. Then prove to your children that you hold yourself accountable, and ask them for their forgiveness. That's exactly the sort of interaction that the Holy Spirit is designed to facilitate and enhance.

FATHER PURE GOLD #1:
Knowing you've done your job

When it comes to being a parent, you *did* do your job, didn't you? If you've got a child who now walks, talks, and generally functions like an adult, then your Primary Business has been attended to. Times between you and your child were rough; times were good; times were sweet; times were bitter—but in the end, you did it.

Just look at that child of yours. That there's an adult. Look at how beautiful, tall, and *capable* your child is! Just look at the wonder you've wrought!

Okay, quit looking at your child with that expression on your face. You're getting all misty-eyed.

Hey! *Hey!* Do you want your kid to think their dad is a mush-cake?!

Ah, go ahead. Grab a box of tissues. It's okay. After all, if you can't get choked up about your own kid, then what *can* you get choked up about? All the birthday parties, Christmases, classes, practices, school events, best friend dramas, worst enemy dramas . . . it's been one full plate, hasn't it? No matter what struggles you, your wife, and your children went through, in the end, you're all still standing and alive, right? (Unless, God forbid, that's not true; unless you have lost a child. If you have suffered that tragedy, may God bless you every moment you're on this earth, because nothing hurts more.)

We tend to focus on either the present or the future. But if you've got a child whom you can tell is going to be all right on their own, then every once in a while you should make it a point to stop and feel the truth of how righteous that makes much of your past.

It's really something to be proud of. You did what you had to do; you did all you *could* do. And it worked! You've now got an adult where once you had a child. That young adult may not be perfect; it'd be awfully weird if he or she were. But you can trust that life will begin educating him or her in all the ways it was never in your power to anyway.

You did your part. You stuck with it. You *made* it.

And because of you, they've made it.

Here's to you, Pop.

FATHER PURE GOLD #2:
Everything you've learned about the nature of love

As Christians we're pretty comfortable with the idea that God is love. We certainly know it from the Bible. It's pretty hard to misinterpret the part in 1 John 4:8 that says, "God is love." First John 4:16 is also quite clear: "God is love."

Makes you feel warm all over, doesn't it?

It sure does! Love *is* easy and sweet and nice and wonderful!

And then we have children.

And then eighteen years go by—and at that point, about the only thing we know for sure about love is that it's positively insane.

For one thing, it can be so emotionally grueling. Love—raw love, the kind most of us only ever feel for our immediate family and dearest friends—isn't it all about snuggly bears and cuddly hugs, is it? Sometimes love can be downright ugly. And that makes sense, given what a short trip it is between love and anger.

Love of someone = fear of losing that person = needing that person = surrendering emotional control to that person = resenting that person = anger toward that person

You know how they say you always hurt the ones you love? Well, that's why, right there. *That* is the ugly side of love.

But you see how it is? Love. Hate. Kindness. Rudeness. Simple, old-fashioned obnoxiousness. It's somehow all part of the same big picture, isn't it? What we find is that everything inside the picture of our lives is painted from the same material: love. And we really understand how true this is when we look back on all the struggles and joys in the years we spent trying our best to create from our children happy, competent, loving, adults.

In the end, *everything* we do with and about our children boils down to love. But really knowing that doesn't come easy, does it? This stuff has to be *learned*. None of us can just *know* how anything works, or how anything really is, until we've had some real experience with that thing. And the more complex something is, the more time and experience it takes to understand it. That's just life.

Well, there's nothing more complex than God. And that means there is nothing more complex than love.

And we middle-aged parents just spent about twenty years taking one *serious* crash course on love, didn't we?

Twenty years down.

And we'll still know our kids for . . . what . . . forty, fifty, more years?

Some course!

FATHER PURE GOLD #3:
Finally understanding exactly what your parents went through

Remember how your parents used to be so wrong about so much Crucial Stuff? Remember how crazy it used to drive you that they could know so little about your life, yet somehow feel qualified to pass judgment and declare rules about *everything*?

Then—*fast forward!*—you were the parent. The buck stopped with you. You became the best Benevolent Dictator you knew how to be.

But sometimes you didn't know what was best. Sometimes you knew you were making decisions for or about your kids without all the information you would have preferred to have. Sometimes you knew exactly what to do. Sometimes you were pretty sure about what to do. Sometimes you winged it and got it right; sometimes you winged it and got it wrong.

But always—well, *almost* always—you were trying.

And how many times during the course of raising your kids did you think, *Wow. So this is what my parents struggled with?* And every one of those times, you became a little more forgiving toward your own parents, didn't you?

Every time you had that thought—every time you were a little more sympathetic toward your own mom and dad—you became a little more Christlike.

What a blessing our children are to us.

FATHER: Movin' On

According to research so recent we're actually making it up on the spot, 92 percent of Christians believe that God has a plan for them. What's obvious about the remaining 8 percent is that they need to start attending church more often—or listening to Christian radio or watching Christian television or visiting Christian Web sites or reading Christian books or magazines.

That God has a plan for us is certainly comforting and inspiring. But that knowledge also compels a question: What exactly is his plan?

Well, we humbly submit that at least a large part of God's plan for each and every one of his followers is . . . to humble us. It's to use the dynamics of our personal lives and character to once and for all get it into our brains and hearts that *he* is God and we aren't.

"Let go and let God" sure does make for one helpful saying on a bookmark or a Thought for the Day desk calendar. But here's what that saying actually means: "Realize that you personally possess no power of any significance whatsoever. Your will means nothing. Realize that *everything* is in God's benevolent hands. Surrender to the Lord!" Not exactly prime bumper sticker material, is it?

One of the strongest things God can use to eventually drive home to a person that they're not in charge of Everything That Matters is to make them a parent. It sure is easy at first, though, to think we're just a notch below him.

God does, after all, create and sustain life.

Parents *pro*create and sustain life.

Creating a human life. Man, talk about power.

Of course, as Christians we are aware that it's not humans but God who wills children into existence; we understand that in having a baby *we* haven't created human life, God has created it through us. But when the time comes to actually hold our newborn infant in our hands, that little life certainly feels as if it fully belongs to us, doesn't it? And for many years after that moment, our children surely do belong to us . . . and God.

Our children are the ultimate co-production!

When it comes to giving and sustaining life, there's hardly any difference at *all* between us and God, is there?

Is there?

Okay, there is. There really, *really* is, of course. And it's through our all-absorbing role as Big Daddy that God (yet again) proves himself *exceptionally* proficient at driving home to us the nature and degree of that difference.

And how does he accomplish that?

By letting our kids grow older, that's how.

With every passing day—every passing moment—our kids grow smarter, bigger, stronger, wiser, more capable . . . and increasingly independent of us. Little by little, our children show us how they don't, in the end, belong to us at all.

But it's even more than that, isn't it? Because what really happens is that every day our children grow more into the very unique and specific person *they* are.

Which is to say, into the person God made them to be.

Which is to say, into someone whom we could never have anticipated at all.

Our children may look like us; they may walk and talk like us. When they're infants, they can even seem like little, perfect replications—or at least reflections—of us. Still, the simple/complex fact is that our children never become who *we* might desire them to be, do they? We don't *form* our kids. They become who God designed them to be. God forms our kids.

In effect, our children develop—or certainly should develop—into the very people they were born to be in the first place. And all we can do is sort of . . . watch that glorious process, that thrilling revelation of God's astonishingly unique means of creation.

One of the things—maybe *the* thing—about raising a child is that it often takes us along a trajectory that begins with our feeling powerful and godlike, and ends with our understanding that the only way to respond to the development and unfolding of a human life is to drop to our knees in humility and reverence to God from whom all such wonders flow.

As fathers, we are so tempted to think of ourselves as absolutely powerful. Bit by bit, our children teach us how little power we have.

If one of God's purposes is to teach us humility, then in the process of parenting, he sure did come up with a great plan.

FATHER: Things to Do

1. Make a list of what you believe to be your father's best qualities, his strongest and most positive personality characteristics. Then go back over each of those characteristics and
   think about what ways you have or haven't manifested those
   same qualities to your own child or children. Do the same
   thing with whatever negative qualities of your father's you
   feel you may have incorporated into your parenting style.
   Then spend some time thinking about where exactly you as
   a father start, and where you as a son end.

2. If you've lately been going through anything that might have
   caused pain for your children, sit them down and apologize
   to them. Make it clear that you understand how you've hurt
   them and that you take full responsibility for that hurt; it is
   absolutely no fault of their own. Talk to them about what
   it's like to be going through midlife; have utter faith that
   one day they'll be very glad you did. Then give them time
   to respond to you—and with all your heart listen to what
   they say.

3. Just like you did with your wife, ask your child (or each
   of your children) to list five things about themselves that
   they believe you're unaware of. Then set aside generous,
   dedicated blocks of time to spend alone with your child
   while he or she tells you about each of the things on his or
   her list. After having done that privately with each child,

gather them together and as a group talk about what was on each of your lists. Encourage much hugging and open-heartedness. In that spirit, consider in turn sharing with them things about yourself that you're pretty sure they don't know. Nothing of any deep psychological import or anything, but just simple things about your past that would help inform their sense of your own life story (a pet you used to have, a part-time job you had during high school, etc.). Help them understand not just who you are, but who you've been.

4. Make a list of what you consider to be your child's weaknesses. Then think about how they might also be weaknesses of your own. If you listed "too quick to talk back," for instance, reflect on whether you are or ever were inclined to talk back. If you believe your child tends to, say, get involved with people or things much too quickly, then consider how much forethought *you* give people or events before joining in. See if going over your list in this fashion doesn't change or affect the way you see your child, or yourself.

5. Write a letter to your child (or to each of your children) in which you tell that child nothing more than what you truly like about them: what you admire, what particular characteristics or qualities of theirs brings you pleasure and why, what you're so grateful to have learned from them about life, why and in what ways you truly respect them. As you're writing the letter, open your heart as you would

if you knew it comprised the last words your child would ever hear from you. Once it's finished and you've signed it, mail it. Wouldn't you have loved to have gotten such a letter from your own father?

A final note (from Steve): One question I'm frequently asked is: How do I honor a father, like the Bible tells me to do, who was so mean to me or was never there? I always say the same thing. Don't make your father the standard upon which you want to be better. If you do, you will focus on him and will become about half a percent better than him. Instead, raise your children the way the Bible tells you to. Raise them as they need to be raised. Each child is unique, and what a shame to raise all your kids in reaction to how your father raised you. Raise them well by first learning how they need to be raised.

Then, honor your dishonorable father in the only way you can. You can't tell people he was honorable; that would be a lie. You can't tell him you honor him; that would only enable the evil or endorse the evil he put upon you. The only way to honor him is to become a man and a father far better than he could ever help you become. Be a husband, a father, and a man about whom people say, "I'll bet his father is so proud of him." Even though your father may never tell you he is proud of you, your heavenly father will be proud that you did not repeat the evil your father placed on you. You rose above it to do and be more than your father would have ever dreamed you could become—and in doing so became exactly what God knew you would become.

FACE FORWARD | 7

SON, HUSBAND, PROVIDER, Father—and, through it all, He-Man of the Universe.

There it is. There's your life.

That's you in (so to speak) a nutshell.

That is one serious Chunk o' Busyness you've been about, isn't it? Can you believe you've *done* all that? Gone *through* all that? *Been* all that?

And can you believe that you're now middle-aged? Whenever these days you look at a picture of you and your dad when you were a kid, isn't it Too Unfathomable that you are now older than he was when that picture was taken? Especially given how much, in your heart of hearts, you still feel like a teenager?

A couple of months ago we all went home to celebrate my mother's eightieth birthday. While I was there, I pulled out some photos of my wonderful father. I looked at pictures of when he was fifty-four just like me. He looked more like seventy (or I looked more like thirty). I was amazed how different life is today. We have so much ahead of us. The line of life is very long for those of us fortunate enough to be alive today.

Life. It's so . . . fundamentally linear.

And it sure ain't over for you yet, is it?

You're a man whose character has been forged by life, and whose future is going to be shaped by God. All you have to do is open the door to your future, take God's hand, and let him lead you through it.

Speaking of God

So now you know (and, of course, knew before you picked up this book) where you've been—which, in and of itself, is invaluable knowledge. But, like all knowledge, it needs to be periodically reviewed. And since it's been at least . . . what, about one hundred words since we last went over it, let's review it one more time. But *this* time, we'll pair each of men's Life Roles with the primary personal characteristic that we believe God, in his infinite wisdom, used that role to teach you.

Those roles, and their Resultant Attributes, are:

He-Man: Integrity
Son: Openheartedness

Husband: Lovingness
Provider: Faithfulness
Father: Humility

So if there's one thing that with all of our hearts we believe that you, Mr. Reader, can say about yourself, it's that via God's Personal, No-Way-Out, Character-Forging Boot Camp, you now know virtually every last thing you or anyone else *could* know about integrity, openheartedness, lovingness, faithfulness, and humility.

And you just don't know about those five qualities, do you? You *possess* those bad boys. At this point each of those qualities is in you like ingredients in a soup.

So now the question is: What's next? To what end are you now going to apply those five Mighty Fine Qualities that are so definitely and irrevocably yours?

You know what you're going to do? Do you know what your life up to this point has been *all* about thoroughly preparing you to do?

To be a complete and absolute **Man of God,** that's what.

That, we say, is the Big Role to which every other "role" you've played in your life has been leading.

He-Man + Son + Husband + Provider + Father = Man of God. That, we believe, is the formula for your life.

Turns out all those preachers, pastors, authors, and calendar makers were right: God *does* have a plan for you! And we're as confident as can be that it is to spend the second half of your life being the man of God for which the first half of your life has so utterly prepared you.

Just look at the five qualities God has been so long drilling into your soul: integrity, openheartedness, lovingness, faithfulness, and humility. *Those* are *the five qualities that describe any man of God! They are* sufficient *for being a man of God!*

Is it just a coincidence that by the time we're middle-aged, we've really got those five qualities down?

WE THINK NOT!!!

And here you thought middle age was about getting fat, losing your wind, and settling down.

It's show time, big guy. The Big Game of your life is now officially on. Not that you haven't been "playing" in that game all along; not that you're not *already* a man of God. But it turns out that, while you were diligently living your life and being the best man of God you knew how, you were being trained for the big leagues.

And guess what? You got the call! You're goin' to The Show!

More than that: You're already *in* The Show!

All that's left now is for you to grab your mitt and take the field.

To that end, then, let's take another look at how each of your five hard-earned character values will enhance your new life as a truer, deeper man of God. Following that, we'll offer you, via our final Things to Do, some solid, fun, practical suggestions for helping you successfully transition from who you are now to who (glory be to God!) you're going to spend the rest of your life being.

Integrity

People tend to think of integrity as a quality that feels great to possess and manifest. Imagine Batman, standing triumphant over one of his fallen enemies, his fisted hands on his hips, his chest puffed out, simply *glowing* on the inside because he knows he has done something admirable and brave.

Now, what's wrong with that picture? It's that you never see Batman that way, do you? It's just not an image of integrity. It's an image of vanity and shallow pride—and vanity and shallow pride is to real integrity what sugar glaze is to a donut: It makes it more immediately gratifying, but it is basically something that's best left aside. A real superhero doesn't wallow in his victories. He gets back to work.

Batman doesn't pose. Oh, he might pause, for just a moment, to allow himself to register the satisfaction of having taken another bad guy off the streets—but then right away he gets back into his trusty Batmobile, returns to his Batcave, and gets busy solving yet another crime.

And that's what we expect Batman to do. He's not looking for accolades or awards or praise from public officials. We know Batman's better than that.

We know he's got genuine integrity.

We know he knows that he's done his best—and that that's enough for him.

Of course, what we don't know about Batman is whether or not he has a relationship with God. We sure hope he does. Otherwise, sooner or later, simply telling *himself* he's a man of

integrity won't be enough. He'll want someone else to validate
for him that he's a good, worthwhile man doing good, worthwhile things.

If he doesn't know God, it's a sure bet that Batman is going
to want to see his name in the newspaper. He'll crave a little of
that warming, bright spotlight. He'll want Commissioner Gordon
to present him with the keys to the city before an applauding
throng of Gotham City citizens.

And from there, of course—from the moment he smiles
and waves for the camera—it'll be all downhill for our beloved
Caped Crusader. Pretty soon he'll be scheduling his own press
conferences. He'll be staging battles with evildoers in such a
way as to put him in the best possible light. He'll hire writers to
put more *pow!* and *zzzzzwap!!* into his fight scenes.

Then he'll start drinking a little—just at night, to help him
sleep.

Cut to the godly man of integrity: He cares only about one
kind of affirmation in this world, the one he gets from God.
And, frankly, that kind of affirmation doesn't exactly amount
to a party being thrown twice a week. It's about as subtle as
subtle gets. God's ongoing affirmation via the Holy Spirit is no
less real for being subtle—in fact, it's *more* real for being so
subtle—but it is, so to speak, a station to which you have to be
perfectly attuned in order to hear from it enough music to keep
you happily dancing.

Relative to the idea of being affirmed as an altogether admirable man—which is to say, relative to the constant affirmation
none of us can help wanting—a man of integrity must live like

a man whose doctor has placed him on a strict weight-loss diet. Such a man may have a *little* fat, and can enjoy a little sugar—but mostly he has to understand that his desire for fat and sugar is a false, harmful kind of desire; that it's bad and works against his higher, nobler interests.

So it is with a man of integrity: He must, of course, register whatever pats on the back come his way—and he may even derive some emotional gratification from those gestures—but basically he has to forget each pat on the back as quickly as the hand that gave it is lifted. That's because the man of true integrity knows how easily the world's gratification can hook him, how quickly it can wrap him in its downward-pulling tentacles. He knows that if he starts thinking he's worth complimenting and appreciating, that he's someone who *deserves* the respect and admiration of others, then by *nature*—by the design and working of Satan himself—he'll begin craving more and more of that exterior, *human* kind of affirmation.

And before too long, the man of integrity knows, he'll just end up being . . . Bad Batman's drinking buddy.

There's a reason that we, as a culture, associate our men of proven integrity with the image of them (in one way or another) riding off into the sunset. It's because we know that genuine heroes don't care what other men (and—a particular challenge—what *women*) think or say about them. They've learned to entirely disregard that sort of input.

They're tuned in to something deeper.

They're listening to station WGOD ("All Holy Spirit, All the Time"). And if that's *not* the station they're tuned in to, a tragedy is in the making, because we know it's only a matter of time before our hero comes riding *back* into town, the sun behind him now, asking around for anyone who wants to join him for a little rabblin' and rousin'.

God can use any man, for any reason—but a man of integrity can't help but be of special value to him. A man of integrity is, in truth, the rarest kind of man. And it's precisely the kind of man you have been training your whole life to be. By this point, you *do* know the difference between right and wrong. And that knowledge means that as you move into the second half of your life, it's time to finally and thoroughly accept the fact that God's been drilling into you: You were born to be a man of integrity.

You were born to always know and act upon what's right in the eyes of God.

Understand and accept that the enemy of the true man of integrity is the wickedly subtle, perfectly seductive, ever-lurking desire to be *recognized* as a man of integrity, and you will be set for every moment that's ahead.

Then you'll have on the whole armor of God.

And then what can hurt you, He-Man?

Openheartedness

The fantastic thing about midlife is that it really is a time of newness. Everything changes in midlife. Your kids are (mostly) grown; the role you play with your parents changes (if not out-right reverses); your physical and emotional relationship with your wife undergoes radical transformations; your relationship to your job or career shifts into a new and different phase. In middle age everything about your life can seem up in the air.

We believe that's because in middle age God *really* wants to get your attention. And he knows he'll have more trouble doing that if you're too enmeshed in a world you've known too long. For a while—for the first whole half of your life—it's critical that you *do* pay attention to your wife, children, parents, and job; throughout that time God is most pleased that you honor those relationships and dynamics by giving your best to each of them. But by middle age those roles have in a sense played themselves out; more precisely, they've changed and no longer require of you what they used to. And that means once you're in middle age you're free—or certainly a lot freer than you've been for a long time.

And *that*, praise be, is when God can really kick up his level of communication with you. Because then you're much more in open Full Reception. No clouds in the way. No buildings. No static. Just you and . . . WGOD.

God is hoping that by loosening all the old ties upon you—by creating around you open space that you haven't known or existed within for a long time—you will be encouraged to bring forth (and possibly r*ediscover*) your original nature: to bring back to the fore of your consciousness the openhearted, happy, spontaneous *boy* nature inside of you.

The problem with "men" is that "men" think they know everything. Not a terribly helpful attitude when it comes to dealing with God. What God wants is a man who has the openness, trust, and sense of spontaneous joy with which kids tend to engage the world. That kind of man—a man who is eager to listen to God, who is without the pride and persona-related hindrances that so often hobble a man who might otherwise dance to God's music—is someone God can really . . . hang out with.

God is *fun*. God wants us to have fun. He wants us to have fun with him. He wants us to be happy. It's *fun* to be happy.

A "man" doesn't spend much time purely rejoicing, running around with the sheer joy of being alive, freely reveling in all that life can be. A "man" doesn't want to look foolish before others or muss up his shirt or . . . whatever. You know what we mean.

A man not truly open to the heart and will of the Lord, a man who is still protecting himself from essentially being out of control—a man like *all* of us are prone to be—cuts too much of himself off from God.

Not good. Not helpful.

Not fun.

God very much intends for the second half of your life to be what *he* wants it to be—which is to say what you, in your heart of hearts, also want it to be. He wants to communicate to you his knowledge of the way your new life should go and be. He wants you thoroughly openhearted to his message for you. No doubting what he tells you. No evaluating it. No second-guessing it. No "Well, lemme study that proposal and get back to you."

Nah. That's no fun. God wants more from you than that.

God wants *less* from you than that. He wants you to tell your All-Knowing Male Persona to take a hike.

It's the dawn of a new day.

And that new day is a Saturday. You know what *that* means, right?

Cartoons, baby!

Lovingness

Love is God's *purest* gift to us. That is part of the reason why it's also the gift from God most likely to make us a little—or a lot—crazy. Love is just so intense, isn't it? One minute it has you feeling sublime and harmonious; the next it has you unable to think straight.

And then one day we fall in true love with someone; and then we marry that someone. And thus do we enroll ourselves in the ultimate, long-term crash course in one-on-one, Can't Live With 'Em, Can't Live Without 'Em interpersonal relationships.

And *then,* before you know it, we are veritable experts on love.

Hmm. What a coincidence it is, that we should become experts on God's single greatest gift to us at the same time God begins making clear to us that he has something very special in mind for the second half of our lives.

And the something special God has in mind for the second half of our lives (in case we haven't been clear enough on this yet) is for us to become true Men of God.

That means living and reflecting as much of *his nature* as possible.

And that means being as *loving* as possible; it means being as open to God's love as you can possibly be.

And that, sometimes, can present just the tiniest bit of a problem. Because whenever we strongly feel God's love within us, what do we do? Well, by virtue of the fact that we are by nature humble and loving creatures, we tend to either send that love right back to God—to love him with the love we just got from him—or we transfer it into love we then feel for another person, or for people generally.

Now, both of those are wonderful responses, for sure. Love really does, after all, make the world go around. But here's the thing: What too often gets left out of our response to God's love is the part where we're *also* supposed to use it to love ourselves.

Extremely corny cliché or not, it's true: We have *got* to love ourselves. If we don't love ourselves as much as God loves us, then it becomes next to impossible for us to love others as much as God wants us to. Not loving ourselves—not personally availing ourselves of God's love—turns *us* into the kink in the hose that stops God's loving water from flowing.

And being kinky is just plain wrong.

We have to let God show us how to love ourselves; we have to accept God's proof to us on the cross that we *personally* are worth the very highest love. We have no choice in this if we're going to get ourselves out of the way of our best relationship with God. You can't really listen to what someone else is saying if you're thinking too much about yourself. It's when you're peaceful and fulfilled that you can forget yourself enough to pay full attention to someone else.

Still. It's hard to love yourself, isn't it? When you . . . *know* yourself as well as you do?

The thing to do is look at it this way: By virtue of your life experience with your parents, wife, and children, what have you learned about love? That it's all about tolerance, acceptance, forgiveness, and patience, right? You've learned that sometimes people you love just do selfish, stupid, and destructive things— but doing those sorts of things doesn't make those people evil or terrible. Now you know it just makes them human. It's what *marks* them as human. And you don't love those people any less because of the times they're weak. In a way, you love them more for those times, because that's when you see them at their most hurt, their most vulnerable.

Experience with people is how your love for them turns from idealized to real. And real is always better than imagined.

Well, that's how you're supposed to love *yourself*, too. Middle age is when you're supposed to look back on your life and, where it's appropriate, let yourself off the hook for everything you've ever done, said, or thought that ran contrary to God's will for you. You *have* to do that. There's no shirking that (wonderfully liberating!) responsibility. Each of us has to look deep and hard within ourselves, and find our regrets—our shame, our embarrassments, the harm we've done, the hurt we've delivered. We need to identify those regrets, take personal responsibility for them, and then confess to God our transgressions related to those regrets.

For the second half of our lives, God wants us clean. He wants us feeling light, emotionally unencumbered, psychologically unburdened. He wants us fully ready to engage and obey. And we can't do that—we're just not *open* to that—if we're in any persistent way feeling bad about ourselves.

You don't want to be the sad-sack at your own party. Especially if it's a party *God* is trying to throw for you. And *especially* if it's a party the Holy Spirit, through you, is trying to throw for the people in your life.

Part of successfully engaging the second half of your life is releasing the guilt or bad feelings you might have about yourself as the result of things you did in the first half of your life. And in order to release that guilt, you've got to confess it to God and let him cleanse you.

Once that's done, you're *free,* baby! Then it's time to get out there and become the Love Machine God made you to be!

Faithfulness

When I (John here) was around sixteen, the father of a friend of mine started hammering paper plates onto a wooden cross that he had made out of two abandoned railroad ties he'd found.

"So," I said to my friend, "your dad's gone insane."

"I know!" she answered. "It's so weird. He's built, like, four of those crosses, or those stick men, or whatever they're supposed to be, and he just . . . attaches stuff to 'em. I think he's having some sort of midlife crisis."

One Saturday afternoon I wandered into my friend's garage and found her father bent over his workbench, gluing red sequins around the edge of a paper plate that I guessed would soon enough join the other sequin-adorned paper plates on a cross. Apparently he'd found a stack of abandoned railroad ties and wasn't going to let any of them go to waste.

"Hey, Mr. Williams," I said. "Whatcha doin'?"

A tall, heavyset African-American man with big, sad-looking eyes but an extremely quick and broad smile, he stopped what he was doing, gazed at me over the top of his reading glasses, and in the smoky, baritone voice of his that I loved so much, said, "Son, I have no idea."

"Hmm," I said. Pretty interesting answer! "Well, it's safe to say that *one* thing you're doing is gluing stuff onto a paper plate."

Mr. Williams threw back his head and roared a laugh so loud I imagined it dispersing clouds.

"Boy!" he said, "You *got* it! You *said* it! That's *exactly* what I'm doin'! I'm gluin' stuff to a paper plate. That much we *do* know."

"Then you're gonna put that plate on one of these crosses!" I said, thinking maybe I was on a roll. But Mr. Williams gave only a polite chuckle, and then turned to look at the large, heavy, coarse cross standing in the middle of his garage by virtue of a cement block into which it perfectly fit.

"Yeah, that's what I'll do," he said pensively. He slowly shook his head, and in a lower voice repeated, "That's what I'll do." While looking at his cross, he seemed to drift off into some deep, inner place.

"Why?" I said in a near whisper.

He turned his head and locked his eyes onto mine. "You really want to know?"

I nodded.

"Because I hear God telling me to do this," he said. He kept his eyes on mine for just a beat before looking back at Cross With Paper Plates. "That's all I know. That's all I'm doin'."

"Wow," I said.

Mr. Williams let out an abrupt, full laugh. "You said it. That's what I keep thinkin' to myself: 'Wow.' But I don't seem to have much of a choice in this. This is one of those times when I've just got to *obey*. I don't know why God wants me to do this. I'm not an artist. I've never done any art at all—not once, in my whole life. Now look at me. Look at this thing I'm doin'." He picked up the little container holding the sequins. "See these? I went into the crafts store, and I didn't even know what I was lookin' for. Had no idea. Just knew there was somethin' in there I was supposed to get. And I just kept lookin' around, shelf by shelf, aisle by aisle, until I saw these. And bingo—I knew that's what I'd come for."

"Boy," I said. "That's something."

He shook his head. "I know I look a fool out here. Got neighbors lookin' at me like I'm crazy, friends laughin' at me." He fixed me with his gaze again. "But you know what? None of that stuff matters. It's a *pleasure* feelin' God movin' through me. Ain' no pleasure like it. If God told me to put on my bathing suit and go up on my roof and start beltin' out 'The Star-Spangled Banner,' I'd do it. Mess *up* the property values around here—but I'd be up there, singin' out my heart!"

And then he let loose with another weather-altering laugh.

Eight years later, Mr. Williams had his artwork (which rapidly evolved from what I saw in the garage that day) in all kinds of banks and office buildings—and even in the main art museum (!!) of the large city nearby.

This was a man who developed an entire second career (not to mention an entire second income; turns out art *pays*) just by listening to—and *trusting* in—what God was telling him to do. When it didn't make sense. When it wasn't based on anything that (apparently) preceded it. When it left him open to all kinds of criticism.

All right, now. Which of the following do you think is the key lesson we're meaning to impart via the Inspiring, True Story of Mr. Williams?

a. Art pays.

b. John Shore was a teenager of startling brilliance and insight.

c. Never throw anything away, and always bring home anything you might ever use, ever.

d. God puts a message in the heart of *every* man in middle age about what he should do in the second half of his life; each man simply has to focus in, listen for as long as it takes to hear that message, and then fully trust it once it's discerned.

e. d, d, d, d, d.

Humility

One of the main things that stops any of us from being the person God most wants us to be is the deep conviction that we already *know* who we are. Midlife is *the* time in our lives when we need to be extremely open to the truth that we have no idea who we "really" are. God knows who we really are.

And God—and God alone—knows who next we need to become.

The challenge, of course, is to forget everything we know about ourselves, to strip ourselves of our notions of who we are—of what we like and don't like, of what "kind" of person we are, of what our strengths and weaknesses are—so that we're then as open as possible to God's reformulating who we are in whatever way he deems right.

You might think of yourself, for example, as a guy who's done very well in business and now wants to semi-retire and spend his time tending his garden and acting as a consultant for worthy Christian nonprofits who could use a little help.

Great!

Except God might think of you as a guy who needs to forget about his garden and *start* a Christian nonprofit that does something to help those apparently homeless teens you saw downtown the other day. You know? Or maybe God sees you as a guy who works twelve hours a day starting and organizing a huge community garden used by people for miles around you. Maybe he sees you as a guy who does nothing but tend to his garden all day, because he knows that what your soul needs is for you to attentively nurture life the way *he* knows you feel deep down it hasn't often enough nurtured you.

Who knows? Maybe he wants you to start nailing paper plates onto things! You just have to be open to whatever God is telling you to do.

And *the* attitude to open you to that input and keep you open is exactly the thing that God most meant to teach us about when he came down to earth as Jesus: humility.

Humility is a word we Christians hear and read all the time. And we tend to associate it with an almost inexpressive meekness: with a bowed head, a supplicant's attitude, an "I'm not worthy" sort of recessiveness. Those things can characterize a humble heart, for sure. But there's also a desperate ferocity to true, living humility that we sometimes lose sight of when we're discussing or thinking about it as more of an abstract quality than as, say, a force that slams us to the floor, puts its foot on the back of our neck, and keeps us on the floor.

Real, complete, and sustained humility is about as contrary to human nature as it can be.

Unless, of course, you happen to be a man of God. *Then* it's a whole new ball game. Because then you know that in Jesus we find exactly what we need in order to feel righteously humble. Joyfully humble. At once eminently powerful *and* abjectly humble.

Thrilled to have that foot on our neck.

Why? What do we have so much more of than any nonbeliever probably *can* have?

Gratitude. It's our *gratitude* for what Christ did for us that strips us of anything as utterly insubstantial and inconsequential as our dinky personal pride.

We want to give it all to God, because he sure gave it all to us. The sun. The moon. Our families. Love. The blood in our veins.

The blood in his.

All of it, given freely, and for nothing but our joy and benefit.

We're all about halfway home now. At this point we've all spent a tremendous amount of time and energy becoming and being the person we *had* to become in order to reach this point.

From here on out—for fun, for joy, for what really is the best life has to offer us—let's stop being the person we (think we) have to be, and start being the person God wants us to be. No matter what that is; no matter who that is; no matter how that is. Let's just be open, stay open, and obey.

And now—since from here on out you're always going to know exactly what to do anyway, you "integritilicious," openhearted, loving, faithful, humble guy, you—here are our parting . . .

Things to Do

Pray

By which we (still) mean "listen." Just listen. As a Christian, the Holy Spirit's in you; that's where and how God communicates with you. That's extremely active, ongoing, purposeful communication, and now's the time to start making sure that you regularly make a point of carefully tuning in to what God is saying. Nothing new in prescribing that, of course: As Christians, we pray all the time. At *listening,* though—at really settling in somewhere quiet and opening up All Receptive Capabilities to whatever message God is piping in, through and around us—we're maybe sometimes not so good. What with all the . . . Alpha Male stuff driving *us* to do all the talking. But it's probably safe enough to guess that in any of our lives, we've done enough talking for . . . um . . . fifteen eternities.

Let's hear what the Word to end all words has to say.

Grieve Over Your Lost Past

Moving on to new and better things is certainly exciting, but it does mean turning your back on what came before. All of the time you spent with your childhood friends; the school classes you were in; the long, hot summer days; the cold nights of winter; the special, private places you used to go; the pets you used to spend time with—all of it is gone. It's a lot to let go of. Of course we don't ever completely separate from our past; this book is all about how critical one's past is to one's future.

But still, it's good to every once in a while hold in your heart the feeling of the totality of your past—and to then lovingly wave good-bye to it, to watch and feel it as it recedes into the shadows of time. The person you used to be is someone you'll never meet again; the places you used to know, as you used to know them, are gone forever. There's reason there to grieve. Let yourself do that.

Make Your Wife the Entire Point of Taking a Vacation With Your Wife

Trust us: We know that as general Marriage Strengthening Advice, you've heard "Take a vacation with your wife" so often it probably sounds to you about like, "Floss regularly," or "Don't drink and drive."

And we're sure that you have taken vacations with your wife. And you guys probably had a great time. But if we could humbly suggest it, what probably *also* happened whenever you and your wife went on vacation is that throughout that trip you remained . . . well, a guy.

Not that that's bad! It's great! Except that, let's face it, sometimes, to a guy, "Take a vacation" translates into "Struggle to be and remain in control over a ton of stuff that's brand-new to you and basically beyond your control."

Well, for *this* vacation, try something really new. Go ahead and pack your usual swimsuit and Hawaiian shirts—but *this* time, leave behind (if not actually tied up and gagged in the garage) your Adult Self.

Forget him. He's been on enough vacations. Let him stay home on this one; he can pick up the mail, keep the lawn mowed, and pace around in the middle of the night worrying about taxes and mortgage payments.

This time, just bring your little Inner Fun Hound. And make sure your wife leaves behind *her* adult self, too. No grown-ups allowed! On this trip, there's no one but two . . . kids with apparently seriously dysfunctional thyroids.

More, make this particular vacation all about your wife. Make it about thoroughly and constantly indulging her inner kid—about paying attention to that kid, and listening to her, and encouraging her to tell you anything and everything she wants to. Make this trip about celebrating your wife's most authentic thoughts and feelings and experiences.

What a pleasure that's bound to be for you—and what a gift to her. Even if all the two of you do is play hooky from your lives and goof around at home for a nice little stretch of time, do it. Make it about her. Throughout the whole vacation, make it clear to her that you have no other agenda but for her to have fun and feel loved.

Now *that's* a vacation.

That will recharge—if not actually reorient—your life.

Do New Stuff

What's the enemy of life—and particularly of middle age? Boredom—being in a rut, never seeing, thinking, or doing anything new. And what's the answer to being in a rut and never seeing, thinking, or doing anything new? *Doing something new!* So do!

One thing we've talked about in this book is how, in the past, in order to fulfill a job or obligation, we've sometimes pushed aside certain aspects of our personality in order to bring to the fore those aspects of ourselves better suited to the challenge at hand. This is a perfectly good and necessary part of life. But in midlife all the bindings of our lives get loosened; midlife is *all* about change. And one of the most important things you can change—or at least explore—is who you are. Or, more exactly, who you became by virtue of the things you did in your life.

We all tend to rely pretty heavily on one or two aspects of our personalities. But inside each of us are the makings of myriad persons we *could* have developed into besides the person we did. All of us have the potential to be just about any kind of person we want to. Well, midlife is the time to explore areas of your personality that have either never been explored or are now lying dormant. It's the ideal time to purposefully mix up your life a little, to change the patterns of who you are and what you do. If you're always the funny guy, then try being the serious guy. If you never go to art films, go see one—one with *subtitles,* even. If you hate country western music, buy yourself some cowboy boots and a ten-gallon hat, grab that filly of a wife of yours, and head on out to the biggest C&W club in your area. Read a book about something in which you'd normally have no interest. Take a class. *Teach* a class.

We're not talking about radical stuff here. We're not saying you should, like, sell your house and go live on a boat. But we are saying that if that sounds like something you *might* like to do, then take a sailing class—or build a model ship, or visit a maritime museum, or do something . . . nautical.

The point is to stretch yourself a little. Because, as you know, we believe middle age is when you're primed to deepen your relationship with God. And that means really listening to God. And God might have very different ideas than you do about who you are and what you should be doing. And you want to be as receptive to that information as possible. Stepping a bit out of your comfort zone—considering new ideas, practicing new behaviors, trying on new ways of thinking and being in the world—enhances that receptivity. It allows God to communicate with you through channels that might not otherwise be open. You can't, after all, add anything to a box that's already locked up. Doing new things will make you more receptive to the input that means the most to you.

Picture Your Future, Plus One

Imagine yourself inhabiting the future that you *most* want for yourself. Picture all the details of exactly where you are in this Future Perfect life of yours; in your mind's eye, capture how everything around you looks, feels, smells. If you imagine yourself on a yacht, envision the clothes you're wearing, what time of day it is, the temperature of the air, exactly where on the boat you're standing or sitting. If you're inside a little log cabin in the woods, see the pictures on the walls, the coffee cup on the table, the view of the trees out the windows. All of it.

Now just *be* in the place of your choosing for a few minutes. Wait until it's as real in your mind as the place you're actually in.

Once you're settled into that moment of your ideal future, imagine Jesus joining you there.

Enter the Lord!

Now: How does it feel, having Jesus in that place? What does *he* think of the future you've made for yourself?

What does he say to you about it?

What does Jesus think about your yacht or your cabin?

If you feel his love and appreciation for the future you've chosen for yourself, you're on the right track!

If you don't feel the pleasure of Jesus as he beholds you in the future place you've imagined yourself, perhaps you need to "recalculate your route"!

Get Healthy

We know: You've heard it a million times before. Yawn.

And yet, the fact of it remains: Every guy in midlife has got to make sure he's exercising and eating right. As long as you're on this earth, you're occupying the great and wondrous machine that is your ol' bad boy of a body—and machines need maintenance.

But as we say: Nothing you don't know.

What it may be helpful to remind you of, though, is that staying in reasonably good shape—staying in good enough shape, in other words—isn't anywhere near as daunting as our media-drenched culture is forever pretending it is. How hard is it to walk for twenty minutes every once in a while? To just sometimes have water instead of soda? To every once in a while leave a fry on your plate? It's not that big of a deal, is it? The thing is to just start wherever you're at. Do anything for your health, no matter how small it is. You know how stuff like that is. You walk one day; you tend to walk the next. Choose water once; you tend to choose it again. The idea is just to *begin*. Do *anything*. Trust that doing more—even just a little bit more—will follow. And don't worry about *when* it'll follow, or how long it'll be until you're ripped like Tarzan. That's how you stop. Working out and eating right is the one area in life where it doesn't pay to think ahead. Just do a little something In the Now, as they say. Trust that the Later will take care of itself.

One other thing: The fitness advice industry never seems to say this, but one primary reason people don't exercise and eat right is because they know they're supposed to. And people *hate* doing what they're "supposed" to do. That's because we associate *having* to do something with someone telling us that we have to do something. And there isn't a person on this planet who doesn't hate being told what to do.

So if you're someone who resists getting in shape, allow us to say that you do *not* have to get in shape. You don't. You have a right to do with your own body whatever you please. Nobody goes to hell because they're too fat. What you do with your body is entirely up to you.

Your getting and staying in shape has nothing whatsoever to do with *anyone* besides you and God. And God loves you—

whether you're fat, thin, lying on the couch, or running on a treadmill. It's difficult to do, but when it comes to thinking about your physical condition you "should" be in, ignore the maelstrom of Beautiful Body nonsense we're all constantly being bombarded with. Listen only to your patient and loving God.

Start/Join a Group of Midlife Men

Again, not the newest of ideas—but, like "Look both ways before crossing," and "Never look any horse at all in the mouth," it's a good one. We men do tend to isolate; yet, by nature, we are also extremely . . . tribe-oriented. For this, go with your inner Drum Thumper. The bottom line is that it's *good* to be around other guys. And it's fantastic to be around other guys who are going through the same thing you are. Midlife is a uniquely intense phase of life; it's wise to share it with others who know firsthand just *how* uniquely intense it is.

Your church, of course, is the natural place to form or join a midlife men's group. If you do that, though, make sure one of the group's ground rules is that you're all totally honest about your midlife experience. Within the group insist that complete (and confidential) candor be the order of the day. Midlife is like the bottom of the ocean during a storm: All *kinds* of stuff gets stirred up. And judging which of that stuff is and isn't "Christian" isn't going to help.

It's *all* "Christian," of course.

In one way or another, every moment of your life is about Christ. The good. The bad. The ugly. The not-bad. The downright beautiful.

Christ in the beginning; Christ in the end.

And Christ, of all places, in the middle.

APPENDIX

GOING FORWARD AT MIDLIFE:
A RECAP

In your role as He-Man of the Universe, say good riddance to:

1. The terrible burden of unceasing expectation that comes with being He-Man of the Universe.

2. Your enduring, ultimately crippling sense of entitlement.

3. Suppressing your emotions.

4. Going it alone.

As He-Man of the Universe, hold onto and build upon:

1. Your understanding of the nature of power.

2. Your true understanding of, and comfort with, responsibility.

3. Your understanding of how, little by little, mountains can be moved.

4. Your legitimate claim to bravery, born of almost countless challenges faced and overcome.

In your role as Son, say good riddance to:

1. Being physically dependent.

2. The assumption that your knowledge and/or understanding is insufficient.

3. Being emotionally dependent.

4. The things your parents taught you about life that were just plain wrong.

5. The things your parents taught you about you that were just plain wrong.

As a Son, hold onto and build upon:

1. The utter, instinctive joy of being a kid.

2. Every life lesson you learned as a boy.

3. The emotional wherewithal it took to survive childhood.

4. The enduring, deeply affective nature of family.

In your role as Husband, say good riddance to:

1. Basically being insane about sex.

2. All the psychological baggage and lies that stop you from being the greatest husband in the world.

3. Taking your wife for granted.

As a Husband, hold onto and build upon:

1. The invaluable time you've spent with your wife.

2. Understanding the true value of compromise.

3. Being your wife's hero.

4. Feeling/knowing how deeply God has always been with the two of you.

In your role as Provider, say good riddance to:

1. Defining yourself by whatever's written on your business card.

2. The crazy-making gossip and personal politics of the workplace.

As a Provider, hold onto and build upon:

1. Knowing that when push comes to shove, you know how to work.

2. The value and joy of true teamwork.

3. Knowing that people ate because of you.

In your role as Father, say good riddance to:

1. The sheer, unending labor of raising young kids.

2. The burden of always having to be Super, Never-Wrong Dad.

3. The burden of all those times you were something less than the Perfect Dad.

As a Father, hold onto and build upon:

1. Knowing you've done your job.

2. Everything you've learned about the nature of love.

3. Finally understanding exactly what your parents went through.

ABOUT THE AUTHORS

Stephen Arterburn is founder and chairman of New Life Ministries—the nation's largest faith-based broadcast, counseling, and treatment ministry—and host of the nationally syndicated *New Life Live!* daily radio program heard on more than 180 stations nationwide. A nationally known speaker, he has been featured on *CNN Live* and in the *New York Times, US News & World Report, Rolling Stone,* and many other media outlets.

Steve founded the Women of Faith conferences and is a bestselling author of more than seventy books, including the multi-million selling EVERY MAN'S BATTLE series. He has been nominated for numerous writing awards and won three Gold Medallion awards for writing excellence.

Steve and his family live in Laguna Beach, California. For more information, go to *www.newlife.com*.

John Shore is the author of *I'm OK—You're Not: The Message We're Sending Nonbelievers and Why We Should Stop; Penguins, Pain and the Whole Shebang;* and coauthor of *Comma Sense*. He also blogs on *Crosswalk.com*. John and his wife live in San Diego.

New Life Ministries

Building Character and Transforming Lives Through God's Truth

New Life Ministries is a non profit organization, founded by author and speaker, Stephen Arterburn. Our mission is to identify and compassionately respond to the needs of those seeking healing and restoration through God's truth.

New Life's ministry of healing and transformation includes:

- *New Life*–our daily, call-in counseling radio program hosted by Stephen Arterburn. To find a station near you call 1-800-NEW-LIFE or go to www.newlife.com. You can also listen online.
- *Counselors*–our network of over 700 counselors nationwide. Call 1-800-NEW-LIFE to find one near you.
- *Weekend Intensive Workshops and Seminars*
  - *Every Man's Battle*
  - *Healing Is a Choice*
  - *Lose It for Life*
- *Chemical Dependency Treatment*–New Life's *Recovery Place* offers a Christian program of treatment for drug and alcohol addiction. Call 1-800-NEW-LIFE to learn more.
- *Coaching*–Our personal coaching program is "Professional Accountability" to come alongside you and give you solution-focused direction.
- *Website*
  - Podcasts and broadcasts of **New Life**
  - Blogs, message boards and chats
  - Our online store, featuring products by our radio show hosts
  - Find workshops and counselors in your area
- *24-Hour Call Center* – There is someone answering calls in our Call Center, 24 hours a day, 7 days a week, 365 days a year.

1-800-NEW-LIFE   www.newlife.com